Changing Policing: Revolution not Evolution

Michael O'Byrne

Russell House Publishing

First published in 2001 by:
Russell House Publishing Ltd.
4 St George's House
Uplyme Road
Lyme Regis
Dorset DT7 3LS

Tel: 01297-443948
Fax: 01297-442722
e-mail: help@russellhouse.co.uk

© Michael O'Byrne

British Library Cataloguing-in-publication Data:
A catalogue record for this book is available from the British Library.

ISBN: 1-903800-4

Typeset by TW Typesetting, Plymouth, Devon

Printed by Cromwell Press, Trowbridge

Russell House Publishing
is a group of social work, probation, education and youth and community work practitioners and academics working in collaboration with a professional publishing team.
Our aim is to work closely with the field to produce innovative and valuable materials to help managers, trainers, practitioners and students.
We are keen to receive feedback on publications and new ideas for future projects.

Contents

Foreword

It is both a pleasure and a privilege to have been asked to write this Foreword to Michael O'Byrne's book *Changing Policing*.

As a Barrister and High Court Judge I was often closely in contact with Police Officers of all ranks all over England and Wales. In the early days of my retirement I acted as Chairman of the Stephen Lawrence Inquiry and in February 1999 the Report of that Inquiry was published by the Government. I have thus had an unusual and varied experience and view of policing over many years, from the outside. Michael O'Byrne has spent almost all of his adult life as a Police Officer, so that he has been intimately involved inside the Service, and he ended his distinguished career as Chief Constable of Bedfordshire.

This perceptive and forward looking book deals primarily with the author's views on the future of policing in our country. It analyses the problems of the past and sets out with admirable clarity the way in which lessons should be learned in many fields. From my own point of view I note with particular approval the realistic and courageous acceptance of the conclusions and recommendations made in the Stephen Lawrence Report, and the author's wise common sense in his approach to the problems of our diverse society.

This book is wide ranging and thoughtful. It is also adventurous and radical in its approach to the challenges of the future. It is born of wide experience and careful reflection upon many years of service. I am sure that it will stimulate much debate, and will encourage much progress in the planning of Police policies and their sensitive implementation as we enter the early years of a new century.

I warmly recommend Michael O'Byrne's book to readers both within and outside the Police Services of Great Britain.

Sir William Macpherson, at Blairgowrie, 2001

Acknowledgements

I would like to thank Alan Williams, Minna Nathoo, Julie Spence and Carole Teifel for their help with various elements of this book. My consistent pillars of strength have been my wife Carole, who has done a wonderful job in proofreading, sub-editing and worrying, and Denis O'Connor who corrected most of the errors in fact and in thinking in the original drafts: those that are left are mine alone.

Preamble

I have spent almost all of my adult life as a police officer in various guises and owe much to the service. It has taken me around the world; educated me; and provided me with a highly satisfying career in which I was able to change jobs about every two or three years: chief constable was the one I did longest and with the greatest satisfaction. I have had the privilege of working with some of the most interesting and committed of people, only one or two of whom could be described as 'challenging'. If every society gets the police force it deserves there must be an awful lot right with British society to deserve the enthusiasm, commitment and dedication that it gets from its police officers. 'The culture', some aspects of which must be changed, also has enormous strengths. It gets things done in a way that other government bodies and commercial concerns can only hope to aim for, with little prospect of being able to achieve it. It is in that context that I would like the thoughts and ideas described in this book to be put.

Michael O'Byrne

Glossary

ABC	Activity Based Costing
ACC	Assistant Chief Constable
ACPO	The Association of Chief Police Officers
APA	The Association of Police Authorities
BCU	Basic Command Unit
BVPI	Best Value Performance Indicator
CID	The Criminal Investigation Department
CCT	Compulsory Competitive Tendering
CPOSA	The Chief Police Officers Staff Association
CPS	Crown Prosecution Service
DAC	Deputy Assistant Commissioner
DPP	Director of Public Prosecutions
HMCIC	Her Majesty's Chief Inspector of Constabulary
HMIC	Her Majesty's Inspector of Constabulary
ICT	Information and Communications Technology
Met (the)	The Metropolitan Police (London)
NCIS	National Criminal Intelligence Service
NCS	National Crime Squad
NHS	National Health Service
NPT	National Police Training
PCA	Police Complaints Authority
PITO	Police Information Technology Organisation
PNC	Police National Computer
RCS	Regional Crime Squads
RUC	Royal Ulster Constabulary

Introduction

. . . this (the setting up of the Royal Commission in 1960) should not detract from the accomplishment of the first century of policing. From a widely hated and feared institution, the police had come to be regarded as the embodiment of impersonal, rule-bound authority, enforcing democratically enacted legislation on behalf of the broad mass of society rather than any partisan interest, and constrained by tight legal requirements of due process. It was achieved by a variety of police organisational strategies but these succeeded only because of the wider social context of working-class incorporation.

(Reiner, The Politics of the Police, 2nd edn. 1996, p73)

Reiner's statement describes the high point the police had reached by the beginning of the 1960s, the decade in which the brief history described in the first chapter begins. The period that followed had two decades of relative failure and politicisation of the service, followed by the final decade in the last century in which it sought to de-politicise and re-legitimise itself in order to restore its position to that described by Reiner. The issues which need to be addressed if this is to be achieved lie at the heart of this book.

Writing as a retired chief constable I am very aware of the need continually to balance criticism with achievement. That there was a fall from grace for the service in the 1970s and 1980s is a statement of fact. That said, the fall, although a significant one and deeply worrying to both society and the service, was not of the magnitude usually described by the chattering classes. Even at its lowest point the service still retained the confidence of a significant majority of the public: a position which can only be looked on with some envy by its critics in the media and politics, whose own position was always, and has remained, at the bottom of any equivalent test of confidence.

The Government has made it clear that it sees a need to introduce even more changes to the police service, although neither the exact nature of those changes nor how it is believed that they will improve the overall level of service to the public is yet clear. What is clear is that there is a dissatisfaction by the Government with the slow rate of change which takes place in any of the large public organisations. What I have found worrying about the

1

changes which have taken place in the last five to ten years has been the lack of debate and involvement of the service in what are seen to be the deficiencies of the service and how the proposed changes will address them. The template set up by Kenneth Clarke in the institution of the Sheehy inquiry, of management by dictat and non-inclusion, has been closely adhered to by Mr Jack Straw in the management of performance and Best Value. My hope is that government has now got through its teenage phase, as far as policing is concerned, of 'knowing all the answers', and has come to the realisation that policing is a complex activity after all, involving a myriad of choices which would benefit from a major debate focused on the policing rather than political issues, if those changes that are needed to improve it are to be identified and implemented.

This book does focus on the deficiencies of the service. If it is to be improved it cannot be done by looking only at its strengths, which are considerable. The patrol officer is in my view the public face of policing and where 'the tyre hits the road'. It is the most complex area of policing yet is delivered by the most junior and inexperienced officers. This will continue to be the case unless and until significant steps are taken to change the reward system and the mechanics of the shift system. Neither of these will be achieved by the current negotiating processes as long as the Police Federation is allowed to retain the whip hand, both nationally and in dealing with individual chief constables.

In dealing with the issues of diversity and organised crime it is clear that the current structure and organisation of the service is less than ideal. The smaller forces find it difficult to bring sufficient resources to bear to have an impact on these areas. A change in size alone will not cure all the problems faced, but it will enable the creation of an adequate infrastructure in every area to at least promise some hope of improvement. It is unlikely in the short to medium-term that the retention of the current structure will do so.

The issues of performance and philosophy are inextricably linked. Policing is unusual in performance terms in that the usual management approach of measurement in line with the maxim of 'what gets measured gets done' is both simplistic and dangerous. Policing is unique in that work in key areas, such as crime detection, necessarily infringes on the human rights of subjects, and those attempting to improve performance must be alert to the need to retain an ethical approach. This would not be easy in any circumstances and the difficulty is compounded in the service by the lack of sophisticated information systems and some of the essential management skills. Neither is the situation helped by the relatively simple-minded approach of politicians, of whichever party, when they give directions without regard to the complexity of policing and the effect that explicit, implicit and subliminal messages have on setting the service's priorities and standards.

That direction-setting arrangement is now in need of urgent and radical review. The changes over the last decade have effectively been a slow process of centralisation. Police authorities and chief constables are in danger of finding themselves in the same position as Charles Handy's frog which is put into a pot of cold water and slowly brought to the boil. Because the changes happen very slowly the frog does not have sufficient awareness of the changes taking place to leave the pot and dies. In the same way the gradual changes which have been introduced over the last decade are in danger of reducing the police authority to the role of budget manager and the chief constable to that of a local authority chief executive. This may have attractions in terms of tidiness for centralised control, but will only be achieved at the expense of reduced operational effectiveness and local accountability.

Although I have tried where I thought that it was necessary or desirable to support my argument with relevant material, I make no apology for the fact that the final product is closer to journalism than to an academic treatise. The aim is to contribute to the debate for the need for change and offer some suggestions on what that change should be, how it can make a difference for the better and how it could be implemented. In this I agree with Huxley that 'the great end in life is not knowledge, but action.' My vision of the service in the 21st century is, to paraphrase Reiner's earlier description, one that moved from being a homogenous white male organisation to one which welcomed and reflected diversity; in which the weaknesses of institutional corruption and racism had been eradicated; which had regained its reputation for political impartiality, and which had succeeded in squaring the circle of continually improving its service whilst retaining the trust of all of its communities in its commitment to safeguard everyone's rights.

Chapter 1: Where we Have Come From

The 1960s: Today's Beginnings

Before we can consider what the future may look like it is necessary to look to some extent to the past, partly to give a perspective on the present and future and partly to identify themes which may either help or hinder progress into the future. The late 1960s has been taken as the starting point for this brief history. This time was selected for a number of reasons. Firstly, by the end of the decade a large number of demographic and sociological processes, which are the basis of today's society, were firmly underway. Secondly, policing changed quite profoundly at the same time, partly in response to these processes, partly in response to the changes in technology and partly because of growing staff shortages.

The demographic changes

The main demographic and sociological changes concerned population dispersal and family breakdown. Immediately following the Second World War both major parties made continuing and increasingly ambitious promises that more and better housing would be provided, especially for the populations of the inner cities. As a result, most of the existing cities expanded significantly into the suburbs, very often creating two new kinds of large estate. The first, which caused little in the way of policing difficulties, was that of the private builder offering families the opportunity to buy their own homes in significantly improved surroundings. The second has been the cause of much commentary and soul searching: it was that of the large council-built estate, usually on the edge of the existing conurbation, which began in the 1950s as relatively low density housing but then had all the benefits of high density, high-rise buildings imposed upon it.

In addition, a significant number of 'new towns' were created. These were usually located well away from the previous centres of population and the planners were given greenfield sites which should have ensured success. The scale of population movement from the inner city to the suburbs and the new towns is best demonstrated by the fact that in 1951 a total of 143,000 people lived in the new towns and by 1969 that had become 1,340,000. Needless to say this migration and population increase had not been accompanied by the same commitment to increasing police numbers or policing facilities in these areas. In addition, both the suburbs and the new towns were highly dependent on cheap and readily available public transport which existed at that time but which has long since disappeared. This meant little to the privately built estates, as the same ability which enabled their occupants to purchase their own house also enabled them to purchase their own transport. It did mean that they contributed to the growth of private cars with the consequential policing difficulties which that created both in terms of road usage and in increasing the number of potential crime victims.

This latter element has had a phenomenal effect on policing. The growth in numbers of motor cars has had two profound effects. Firstly, it has been possible for people to live in one area and work somewhere else, sometimes quite far away. This has greatly increased the speed of break-up of the extended family as children, seeking to better themselves and their position, quickly moved away from both the family home and the family neighbour-hood. This meant that the support for children, parents and the elderly which was readily available in early post-war society had already begun to disappear. In addition, the availability of motor vehicles has meant that criminals are no longer restricted to their own locality but have the ability to range far and wide. This was a paradigm shift in crime methodology which completely undermined the traditional policing approach based on 'local knowledge', i.e. knowing who was criminally active locally by either recognising their m.o. (modus operandi), or using local informants to find out.

Staying with the demographics, two other issues became firmly estab-lished in British culture at that time. The break-up of the nuclear family began to become apparent. Divorce was becoming more common and it was becoming less and less rare for couples to live together either on an uncommitted basis or as an agreed precursor to marriage. It is unlikely that anyone at the time anticipated just how far this trend would go. The same is true of the second issue: that of drugs. The rock and roll and hippy decade had firmly established drug taking as part of an acceptable way of life for a fairly large number of people. It had moved from the position of being a rather exotic thing that the rich and idle did, to being something which a large number of young people experimented with and which a significant number then adopted as part of a lifestyle.

The police

Meanwhile, things were changing at an unprecedented rate for the police service. The 'baby-boom' which followed the war had now become young adults. The whole attitude to authority was changing and it was becoming acceptable, if not expected, to challenge rather than accept. The dispersal of the population to the suburbs and away from city centres generally meant that the traditional beat system could no longer work. The magnitude of this change cannot be underestimated. Policing was traditionally based on a system of beats staffed by uniformed patrol officers. This had been the case for over 100 years. The whole management process and service delivery was built on it and it visually represented the public's expectation of policing. (Indeed it is still part of the British policing 'mystique' and is seen as the panacea for all policing problems).

The growth of the motor vehicle had been reflected in police practice with a compensating growth in the police use of cars. These however were still relatively small in number and they were seen to be a support for the beat system rather than a key component of service delivery. Technology was also beginning to change the nature of police work. The expansion of the telephone system in the 1060s (although miniscule in relation to the recent explosion in telephone ownership due to mobile telephones) had made the police more accessible and had increased the demands for police response.

The growth in the availability of consumer goods meant that there was much more there to steal and property crimes grew at an unprecedented rate:

- 461,435 in 1950
- 743,713 in 1960
- 1,133,882 in 1965
- 1,498,700 in 1969

Young people were becoming involved in crime more often and at a younger age and it was recognised that the better way forward was to keep them out of the criminal justice system, at least for the first offence. This led to the institution of the police caution. This again was a major change, the significance of which is often lost. It was the first formal step in which the police recognised that the service had a role other than enforcement and it was the first formal step in which the line between executive (police) and judicial (magistrates) decision-making overlapped.

The internal forces of change were just as powerful. Following on the Royal Commission of 1960–62 came four significant changes. Firstly police pay was reviewed objectively in light of the need to provide a professional service. This led to a significant improvement in police pay and conditions of service. It also meant that providing the police service had become significantly more expensive and this may have led to the staffing problems of the late 1960s. Secondly, the number of forces was radically reduced during the period 1964–68 under the home secretary, Mr Roy Jenkins. During this time all of the borough and small county forces disappeared, reducing the numbers from 126 to 47. Thirdly, police authorities were created by statute with the responsibility to provide an effective and efficient police service. In most cases they remained a part of local government, but the statute gave them the ability to set a budget based on the policing need rather than one which was determined in the light of other county or borough council needs. It also clarified to some extent the relative positions of the police authority and the chief constable. The final change, which is still the subject of much debate today, was the introduction of a statutory complaints system.

The combined effect of all of these changes created a service which was required to provide a much more professional level of service. The reduction in the number of forces, combined with the establishment of police authorities, opened the way to selection based on merit and potential rather than local patronage and the appointment of the more able to police leadership (a lesson for today?). The new forces were however now more remote from their community base (another lesson for today?): this was true for both chief officers and police authorities.

The service's response to the combination of a growing volume of demand and the increased complexity of the policing task, neither of which was matched with a complementary growth in resources, was 'unit-beat policing'. The system had been introduced in Lancashire by the very forward-looking Chief Constable St. Johnson. Instead of having one officer per beat supplemented by some car patrol, a number of beats were amalgamated and allocated a patrol officer based in a vehicle called a 'panda car' (because of the marking). The idea was that the officer used the car to get around the larger area and that he (and at that time it was a 'he') would get out from time to time and carry out foot patrols; the distinctive marking would make him visible to the community. The use of the car enabled the officer to deal more effectively with the mobile criminal, the larger patrol area and the increased workload.

There were four additional features. Firstly, each of the larger areas would also have a dedicated 'home-beat' officer who was intended to carry out foot patrol and build up community contacts. Secondly, an intelligence system was instituted to gather and analyse information coming from the panda and home-beat officers. This was based in the main police stations and was centred round the new post of 'collator'. Thirdly, the officers were issued with a personal radio which massively increased their ability to communicate both with the station and with other patrol officers. Fourthly, each of the large areas was supposed to have a dedicated detective. This latter feature was the least likely to be formally instituted, or if instituted, was the first to be abandoned.

It is accepted that the system was never properly evaluated although the early indications appeared to be favourable. For whatever reason, most likely that of cost, the concept was picked up enthusiastically by the Home Office and was more or less forced on the service nationally. Along with the stick of coercion came the carrot of additional finance for cars and radios. No doubt this latter feature meant that it was instituted more enthusiastically than is normally the case for change on this scale. The changes were welcomed by patrol officers for two reasons: firstly, patrolling in cars was seen to have a higher status than on foot. It satisfied the policing need in the eyes of the officers as it enabled them to respond quickly to the increasing calls from the public and to deal more effectively with an increasingly motorised criminal. Secondly, the advent of the personal radio significantly improved officers' safety and gave the patrol officer immediate access to facilities such as intelligence reports which were based at the station, where previously he needed to wait until he had an opportunity to return to the station, an act which was not encouraged by supervisors and was difficult if patrolling a more remote beat. It appeared to be a 'win-win' solution for everyone at the time. The community got a more responsive police; the officer got better job satisfaction and increased safety; police leaders were given a framework to replace the beat structure, and it appeared to be cheaper than the traditional approach. The fact is that it did achieve all of these things. What it did not do, and what it could never have done, was return society to the halcyon days of the 1930s and the early 1950s where there was a more pervasive police presence in a more orderly and cohesive society with a lower level of criminal activity and a higher level of community and family support.

The 'Catch-22' of the situation is that in successfully managing the consequences of the changes of the 1950s and 1960s within the terms of reference then open to it, i.e. little additional funding and retention of patrol as the core element, the police service had subscribed to a philosophy that in the future would ensure that it always failed in the eyes of a public which increasingly associated security and confidence with foot patrol: a point of view still continually reinforced by politicians' use of the soundbite panacea of 'more officers on the beat'. The key measure of success in policing was to become not only what happened to crime, response and dealing with quality of life issues, but also the visible police presence on the streets. This had become a symbol of a state of orderly society that no longer existed but which was seen as the ideal. Everyone involved, chief constables, the Police Federation, local and national politicians, used the same measure for different reasons. All played on the emotional response of the public to the idea that a police presence meant safety and re-assurance and that somehow the model based on foot beat patrols was both affordable and effective, despite the fact that it was clearly not affordable, nor was it the most cost-effective way of delivering policing services to the community within the budget actually allowed. When this is added to the real failures of the 1970s and 1980s, the really surprising thing is the extent to which the service has remained so popular and has retained such a high-level of public support.

The 1970s: Feet of Clay Exposed

The police had experienced a halcyon period of public support and had a reputation for being the 'best in the world' throughout the period from the late Victorian age to the late 1960s. As society itself began to experience major change, that same change began to be reflected in its view of the service. The 1970s saw a society that was changing at an unprecedented rate. The moral norms were being questioned at every turn and not just by the young. Cohabitation was beginning to make a serious challenge to marriage, the general view on drugs was a confused one with little in the way of intelligent debate: affluence was beginning to bring its collateral problems of crime and, to cap it all, confidence in the service was seriously undermined by a series of failures throughout the decade.

In addition, the internal management of the service was undergoing massive changes in both structure and style. In structural terms it had gone from 126 forces in 1964, most of which were based on relatively small and homogenous areas and communities, to 43 in 1974, the biggest of which outside London had over 5,000 officers and the smallest around 900. These changes led to long periods of internecine warfare at senior management level as the new forces 'bedded in' and different cliques from the older forces fought for superiority. This led to real difficulties in operational capability at street level. For example, the new Thames Valley force was divided into divisions which did not match the local political divisions in an attempt to break down the five forces that it now encompassed: an attempt that had limited success as 20 years later officers would say that they were retiring from Buckinghamshire, Berkshire etc, and not Thames Valley. In style terms the change from foot to mobile patrol as the core service, together with the introduction of personal radios, meant that the previous management style, which was in the main hierarchical and mechanistic and was more clearly aligned to a military rather than industrial model, could no longer cope. Although the training given to managers and supervisors tried to deal with this, it is clear that many middle managers had real difficulty in adjusting to the change and, as will be argued later, it is this inability to predict and anticipate the effects of change which has been a constant feature in police management since the 1960s. All of this was happening against a background of relative decline in conditions of service and pay and a gradual reduction in police numbers and quality of entrants (especially in London), which needed to wait for the findings of Lord Edmond Davies in 1979 to reverse.

The key change which this brought about was the way in which patrol and detective officers gradually became unaccountable for their work. On a foot patrol based system, officers were restricted to very small areas of patrol and had to account for themselves by 'ringing in' from police boxes strategically placed around the division. If anything happened on their beat they were expected to be aware of it and to have acted in response. (It was not unknown for officers to be called back from sleep after night duty to account for a break-in which had occurred and which they had not found in the course of the patrol). Everything they did had to be noted as it occurred and the main form of supervision was through sergeants and inspectors meeting officers on patrol and countersigning their notebooks. The move to mobile patrol made this completely impracticable. The officers were implicitly expected to adopt a more tactical and problem-solving role, but were not given the intelligence systems, training or management support necessary to make this approach work.

As far as detectives were concerned, the major change was from organisations which were small and local and in which senior officers were a part of the community that was policed. They could thus become aware of what was going on either through direct supervision or through feedback from the community. Whilst this had its difficulties, and some of the failures of this decade were due to collusion between supervisors and constables, the move to larger forces tended to remove the CID to the larger stations and led to the creation of specialist units, inadvertently creating a level of anonymity which defeated the supervisory processes of the time.

How did these failures in leadership manifest themselves? The three key areas were those of corruption, the control of public order and the prevention and detection of terrorism.

Corruption

The decade began with the infamous exposure of Metropolitan Police corruption by *The Times*. Two reporters from *The Times* worked with known criminals in order to obtain evidence of corruption on a number of

Metropolitan Police detectives, some at a relatively senior level. They secured unimpeachable evidence through surveillance and tape recording interviews. The key failure in leadership was how the case was handled. The initial response was to defend the officers and question the reporters. It took a significant amount of effort on the part of *The Times* to keep the story alive and to have it taken seriously. The case made it clear that corruption of this type was routine and pervasive yet the initial response was one of defence and cover-up. The appointment of Sir Robert Mark as Commissioner moved the issue on in the Metropolitan Police but it is clear that other chief officers thought that this was a 'Met' problem and did not affect their forces. It is clear from what happened subsequently with the West Midlands Crime Squad that this was a false assumption.

Although Mark introduced reform on a wide scale, subsequent corruption scandals involving the Drug Squad and the Obscene Publications Squad dramatically demonstrated both the scale of the problem and the limited impact that any one chief officer can have. The most infamous case of the 1970s was that of 'Operation Countryman'. The case had two aspects other than corruption: how success can turn quickly to failure and the efficacy of 'outside' investigations. In the early and mid 1970s the Met developed so-called 'supergrasses' who gave evidence against other criminals on a scale never before contemplated, in return for relatively light sentences and new identities. It proved to be a highly effective strategy in dealing with serious criminal gangs, particularly those involved in armed robbery. However, it rebounded on the force when the same approach was used against corrupt police officers.

The inquiry was initially directed against officers from the City of London but was quickly expanded to include the Met. The operation was run initially by the Dorset police and then by the chief constable of Surrey. At its peak over 80 officers from various forces were investigating over 200 from the City and the Met. It resulted in the prosecution of two officers. The scale and cost of the inquiry was such that the service was seen to be either covering up or incompetent. The latter was reinforced by the nickname, 'The Swedey', that the Met officers gave the inquiry team. Whilst there is no doubt about the integrity of the chief officers involved, the outcome was one which undoubtedly undermined confidence in the abilities and leadership qualities of chief officers in the minds of both the public and members of the service. During the same period the Met's own investigations resulted in over 100 officers being dismissed or required to resign (*The Job* 18.8.82).

The three key issues were:

1. That corruption was still seen as one dimensional and was only associated with taking money for favours: what became later known as

'noble form corruption' i.e. perverting the course of justice in order to ensure that known criminals were convicted, was not dealt with at all and continued to be tolerated in the service as a whole. The extent of this would not become clear until the reversal of verdicts in the late 1980s and early 1990s.

2. The almost insuperable difficulty that the burden of proof presented to investigators. The police discipline system uses the same burden of proof as the criminal law, i.e. beyond a reasonable doubt. In almost all other employment the test is the civil one of balance of probabilities. This difficulty was compounded by the 'double jeopardy' provisions of the discipline code which meant that if an accused officer was not proceeded against by the Director of Public Prosecutions (or later the CPS), or was acquitted at court, he could not be proceeded against under the discipline provisions, i.e. put in jeopardy twice on the same issue. The Police Federation's view that the officer was in jeopardy twice was fatuous. One decision, that of the DPP or jury, was about criminal liability, the other, discipline, was about suitability as a police officer, i.e. employment. The injustice created by this feature was that the DPP/CPS decision not to proceed was based on the likelihood of convincing a jury of the officer's guilt. This has always proved to be difficult even in the light of overwhelming evidence and the decision threshold was necessarily high. The decision threshold for appearing before a chief constable, the disciplinary authority, would always be significantly lower. Despite this both of these features were accepted by chief constables (and the Home Office) and continued to be defended by them until the mid 1990s.

3. The experience raises serious questions about the effectiveness of outside investigators, especially when they do not fully understand the culture of the force being investigated and where malpractice on a serious scale causes them to be confronted by a wall of silence and minimal co-operation.

The control of public order

There is no other area of policing which so crystallises the tensions created in a democracy as that of attempting to balance the rights of the many to public tranquillity with those of the minority who wish to draw attention to their cause by way of public demonstration. It would appear that the greater the gap created by the political issues of the moment, e.g. between animal rights activists and those who support experimentation, the harder it is to achieve the necessary balance: using the same group as an example, balancing the right of the activists to demonstrate against those of the laboratory workers to go about their business unhindered. This in turn appears to lead to a high level of frustration in the minds of the minority and a greater willingness on their part to turn to violence, probably compounded by the alignment, in their eyes at least, of the police with the government of the moment where the issue is more overtly political, e.g. the miners' strike. The key to success when this occurs lies in the twin pillars of leadership and accountability.

Leadership in this area is in two parts; firstly there must be political leadership by government. It must declare, clearly and unequivocally, what it seeks to achieve and why, and to describe publicly what it sees as the police objective. In the absence of this it will be almost impossible for the police to know where consensus lies and how far the service is expected to go in enforcing the will of the majority. This is key, as the control of disorder inevitably requires a very public use of force and it appears to be a feature of British society, certainly of reporting by the media, that there is some expectation that when politically motivated violence erupts it can somehow or other be met and controlled by persuasion alone. This was very powerfully the case in the 1970s.

Secondly, there must be clear service leadership. This is necessary in order that operational commanders know exactly what they are to achieve; how they are to achieve it; what level of force they are expected to use and at what point to concede the ground to the demonstrators rather than use a level of force above that defined level. The absence of this clarity will inevitably lead either to the service using an unacceptably high level of force or to conceding the ground where the public's expectations are that they should have held it.

In the 1970s neither of these conditions were satisfied. The Heath Government was never quite clear what it wanted to achieve in terms of trade union control. It was seen to carry out a number of 'U' turns and gave little direction to the service on its expectations on the control of disorder. This was followed by a weak Labour administration which had to struggle with a small majority and which, in a different way and for very different reasons, also had an ambivalent view on trade union control. In these conditions it was difficult for the service to match the significantly increased levels of resistance and violence that it met in trying to control both political (mainly against the war in Vietnam) and trade union demonstrations. Throughout the decade it moved from the Mark theory of 'winning by appearing to lose' (the Grosvenor Square riot in 1968), through 'losing by not being able to win' in trying to keep open the Saltley coke depot in 1973; through to 'losing by manifestly not being allowed to win' in Red Lion Square and Southall. In between times the Metropolitan Police were subjected to unnecessary public ridicule by being expected to deal with serious rioting around the Notting Hill carnival equipped only with dustbin lids and empty milk crates.

The service was very slow to react to the change in the public attitude to disorder in both legal and technical terms. At the Red Lion Square inquiry a Metropolitan Police deputy assistant commissioner gave evidence that the police officers under attack could only use their batons as weapons of defence. This ran full in the face of all of the common law on the suppression of riot and disorder. This not only allowed the use of aggressive force in order to subdue riots, but actually created a common law misdemeanour of failure to do so through the lack of will to restore order. (The mayor and captain of the militia in Bristol in 1831 were imprisoned for such a failure.)

The rank and file of policing were thus left high and dry by their leadership. They were not allowed to do the common sense things which they knew would be effective and those same leaders did very little to equip them to carry out what appeared to be the only alternative strategy, i.e. of standing by and absorbing punishment. Protective shields were not available until the late 1970s and the risible attempts to convert the policeman's helmet into an effective piece of protective equipment left officers exposed to unnecessary injury purely in order to avoid anything that looked paramilitary. The trend and nature of the change was clear; the response, even acknowledging the benefit of hindsight, was short-sighted and inadequate. The real penalty was to be paid for this in trying to control the extensive urban rioting that occurred in 1981. To compound matters, little or nothing was done to win the political debate or to obtain publicly declared clarity of direction from government.

Terrorism

There is no doubt that terrorism presented one of the biggest challenges to police leadership in the latter part of the 20th century. Although there was an international aspect to it, the debate here will be restricted to Irish nationalist terrorism. The initial mainland police reaction to IRA terrorism can only be described as very poor in almost every respect. Any study of Irish nationalist terrorism would have shown that the terrorists have a willingness to operate on the mainland if they think that this will serve their political ends. Given that the troubles in Ulster had been going on for two to three years, depending on which start point is taken, it is difficult to conclude other than that the intelligence systems of both the Special Branch and the Security Services were inadequately developed to deal with the attacks when the inevitable did occur in 1973. Although the service quickly developed better techniques for evacuation and scene handling (thus the more effective recovery of forensic evidence), the delay between the existence of the threat, the outbreak of mainland attacks and the development of effective intelligence, in either the preventative or investigative sense, was very slow.

If the opposition could have been described as highly intelligent, well-organised and highly effective in the development of disinformation and circumvention of police methods, there could be some excuse for this. The opposite appeared to be the case. One of the very few successful anti-terrorist operations was that which culminated in the Balcombe Street siege in 1975. In this operation the pattern of previous terrorist activity led the Metropolitan Police to believe that another attack was imminent and the area where the attack was expected was flooded with plain clothes police officers. The terrorists attacked a restaurant with automatic machine gun fire and were then pursued by the police in the area. In the course of the chase they abandoned their automatic weapons and eventually took refuge in a flat in Balcombe Street. At the end of the five day siege the four terrorists surrendered peacefully. A significant feature of this operation was the stupidity of the terrorists in developing a pattern of attacks which allowed the police to anticipate the next event, in abandoning their automatic weapons which may have enabled them to fight their way out of any situation (armed police units were usually only equipped with handguns at that time) and in the absence of any fallback plan for a getaway should the attack go wrong. Indeed Sir Robert Mark commented in his autobiography: *'our assessment of the intellectual capacity of the bombers was not mistaken'* (in their tendency to follow an identifiable pattern) and, *'Once holed up in Balcombe Street by their own stupidity as much as anything else . . .'*

Despite this there were relatively few successes in the decade and it would appear that in those cases where the police were apparently most spectacularly successful that success was not built upon ethical investigations. As well as ruining the lives of the persons arrested, they would come back to haunt the service in the 1990s. Although society as a whole, and the media in particular, all played a part in the hysteria which followed the bombings in Guildford, Birmingham and elsewhere, the role of chief officers was to balance the clear concerns of the public with the rights of suspects. It is clear that they failed to do so.

The 1980s: Failure and Politicisation

The inner city riots

The decade began with the first serious street riots outside London in the St. Paul's area of Bristol. The initial reaction was that this was a 'one-off' and was unique to the particular problems of that area in that city. Little if anything was done to learn from the Bristol experience to prepare other forces for what might happen to them. In the following year serious rioting broke out all over England; first in Brixton in London, then in Toxteth, Liverpool and then on a lesser scale in a number of other cities. The more serious rioting was in Brixton in April and July and in Toxteth in July where it took several days for order to be restored and where the Merseyside force needed assistance (mutual aid) from a large number of other forces.

In dealing with these disturbances it was clear that very little had been learned from the experiences of the 1970s. The equipment was totally inadequate; the remodelled police helmet was ineffective and the long shields, while providing some protection, also created a target and significantly reduced police mobility, a key factor in regaining control. The radio systems were designed for one-to-one communication and could not cope with the network requirements of a paramilitary structure. (This is still the case some 20 years on.) The tactics assumed that a police presence in itself would restore control. They could not cope with sustained attacks by determined crowds and the use of weaponry such as scaffolding poles and petrol bombs.

The situation was exacerbated by the chief officer response which raised the usual conspiracy theory that left-wing activists and anarchists were at the root of the problem. In this they followed in the footsteps of their American colleagues in responding to their inner city riots of the mid and late 1960s. As the inquiry under Lord Scarman would come to find, (just as the Kerner Commission in the USA had done), the core issues were those of social deprivation and insensitive and unimaginative policing. Although the serious rioting seemed to be restricted to 1981 it was accepted, at least in London and Liverpool, that the potential for serious disturbances continued throughout the early 1980s.

This culminated in the recurrence of serious rioting in Birmingham and London in 1985. In the Handsworth area of Birmingham a riot broke out, (the day after a successful street carnival), in which two Asian shopkeepers died as a result of staying on their premises in the hope of protecting them from looting and which were subsequently set on fire. In London, on the Broadwater Farm Estate, a violent riot resulted in the death of Police Constable Keith Blakelock. The significant difference in the reaction to these riots and those in 1981 was the way that the black youth involved were described as being clearly criminal, and the way in which the riots were depicted as being part of a concerted attempt to keep the police out of the area in order to allow criminal activities, especially drug dealing, to take place. Almost all the commentary ignored the possibility that the actions of the youth may have been caused by their ghettoisation, frustration caused by high unemployment, alienation and what they saw as police harassment. It was almost as if Lord Scarman's inquiry had never happened.

The way that inner city disorder was dealt with demonstrates two key factors. Firstly, the trends in violent protest were clear. The fact is however that, under pressure, the equipment, the training and the tactics remained inadequate. Secondly, despite having the benefit of Lord Scarman's inquiry and its detailed findings, the tendency for the remainder of the decade was to treat inner city disturbances as being criminal rather than recognise the impact of deprivation and discrimination. Although Lord Scarman acknowledged that the police did more to implement his recommendations than any of the other agencies, the fact is that the policing response to the complex issues of the inner cities generally remained as unimaginative as he had described in his report.

The Police and Criminal Evidence Act

By the mid to late 1970s it was evident to any informed commentator that the situation regarding suspects in English law was no longer tenable and that change was in the offing (O'Byrne, 1978). In 1984 that change was made with the introduction of the Police and Criminal Evidence Act which introduced significant additional safeguards for suspects, both in the street where police powers to stop and search were finally defined in law, and in the police station where the rights of the suspects were also similarly defined. These statutory changes were backed by detailed guidance in codes of practice. All in all the service was given about two years formal notice of the changes in order to be able to review practice and to ensure that adequate training was given to all personnel.

Despite this the service in the main dealt poorly with the introduction of this major change in legislation. Many officers did their best to ignore the constraints where they cut across previously accepted practice. The CID were particularly poor at coping with the changes and were quick to blame the Act for the drop in the rate of detections and in the unwillingness of suspects to talk to them and to admit further offences. Although the training which they had been given dealt fairly effectively with the technicalities of the law, almost no training was given in how they should adapt their methods of investigation to cope with the changes. For example, the reduction in the time a suspect could be held meant that more of the investigation needed to take place before the arrest was made. Similarly, suspects with access to legal advice were only likely to confess if the police evidence was strong, if not overwhelming. Both of these factors required significant changes in CID practice, neither was planned for and it took some considerable time for the need to be recognised and implemented.

The overall attitude of the CID to the change is exemplified by the case of *R v. Samuels* which revolved around the admissibility of a confession made by the suspect while denied access to legal advice. In this case the officers had refused the suspect access to a lawyer on the grounds that notifying a lawyer may have warned accomplices of the arrest and that if given legal advice it was unlikely that he would say anything at all. The suspect's mother was already aware of the arrest and could have thus warned any accomplices. There was no evidence that the lawyer was other than reputable and would be willing to assist the suspect in warning anyone else, and giving the suspect access to legal advice on how to reply to police questions lay at the heart of the Act's provision. In these enlightened times when the United Kingdom has finally made the European Convention on Human Rights accessible to every subject in its own courts, the police case appears incongruous. However, it was pursued seriously at the time and even got some judicial support. The case was notable in that the Court of Appeal applied some of the thinking behind the American doctrine of 'fruit of the poisoned tree', i.e. if any act in a series of acts is unlawful all of the evidence obtained as a result of the series is inadmissible, and the confession was ruled inadmissible. This was a sea change in judicial attitude to the admission of confession evidence as up until then judges had admitted confession evidence despite overwhelming evidence of police mispractice. The judgement changed the whole police approach to ensuring compliance with the new codes of practice as it was clear that non-compliance would make evidence inadmissible. (The effect the judiciary has on police ethics will be dealt with in more detail in Chapter 4.) This judgement was followed in a number of other serious cases, some involving murder, and probably did more than any other factor to cause the service to take the provisions of the Act seriously, at least in the case of arrest.

This was again a change that would clearly have a significant impact on police effectiveness, where there were clear indications that change was imminent (and necessary) and where the steps to be taken to minimise the disadvantages of the change were clear, yet where it took a period of four to six years after the implementation of a thoroughly publicised Act for the service to make those necessary changes. The cost was that the courts were not allowed to deal appropriately with serious offences, that victims were let down and that confidence in the service was further eroded.

Converting resources into performance

Throughout the 1980s the amount of resources dedicated to policing grew faster than nearly any other public service. It is accepted that much of this additional resource was due to the effect that the Edmund Davies formula had on police pay. The inquiry by Lord Edmund Davies in 1979 into police pay and conditions led to police pay being more or less doubled in two years and then linked by formula to rises in the national rate of pay of skilled workers. However, even when that was taken into consideration there was a significant increase in the actual resources dedicated to policing in this period. There is no doubt that these additional resources, and the support of the government which they reflected, enabled the police to deal with the miners' strike, the firefighters' strike, the ambulance strike and the prison officers' dispute. However, as far as the average member of the public was concerned, if success was to be measured by the rate of increase or decrease in crime or in detections, the police clearly failed to convert the additional resources received into improved performance.

Between May 1979 and January 1988 the police strength in England and Wales had risen from 109,998 to 122,131, an increase of 11 per cent. In London the Metropolitan police had grown from 22,225 to 27,449. Throughout the period police pay had usually risen in excess of inflation which should have enabled the service to recruit better quality candidates. However, during this same period crime rose inexorably from 2,537,000 in 1979 to 3,830,000 in 1989. In 1983 the Home Office issued Circular 114/83 on *'Efficiency, Effectiveness and Economy'*. This was probably one of the best guides produced by the Home Office and is a model of brevity and clarity. It described in simple understandable English what forces had to do in order to ensure that they were achieving the three 'Es'. At the same time a number of forces and Her Majesty's Chief Inspector of Constabulary (HMCIC) became interested in the approach advocated in *Policing by Objectives* by Lubens and Edgar. Thus the service cannot say that it was short of effective guidance on how it could convert these additional resources into improved performance. The concept was taken up with some enthusiasm by Sir Kenneth Newman, the then Commissioner of the Metropolitan police, and quickly spread throughout the service.

The key difficulty was that most forces concentrated on the development and publication of plans that looked good, rather than on the implementation of plans which were effective. (It has to be said that this follows exactly how industry and commerce initially reacted to the same concept.) The failure in policing was that the time that it took to mature in this area was not a matter of two or three years but, in fact, well over ten. Indeed, a significant number of forces have yet to institute the rigour of setting achievable targets, developing effective systems of measurement, implementing effective monitoring and then reviewing what has been achieved in the light of the target. It is not clear even now that the majority of senior management in the service (superintendent and above) understand the concepts that underpin targets, measurement and review, nor, it must also be said, do the HMIC, the Home Office and, to a lesser extent, the Audit Commission.

Police discipline

The one constant which followed the service through the 1960s, 1970s, 1980s and indeed into the 1990s, was a lack of confidence in the system for dealing with complaints against police officers, especially when they involved serious allegations of crime or malpractice. It is still a feature of today's service, with yet again new proposals by the government to set up an independent body which will be responsible for the actual investigation into serious allegations rather than the more limited role currently played by the Police Complaints Authority (PCA) which supervises investigations carried out by police officers. The difficulty at the heart of the old discipline regulations was that the burden of proof was the same as in criminal law, i.e. beyond a reasonable doubt. Given the nature of the work, the type of people that police officers deal with, the fact that most confrontations are in a one-to-one situation and that the complainant is more likely to be outnumbered by police officers rather than the opposite, it is unlikely that complainants will be able to cross this very high threshold.

The change in the 1980s which crystallised the level of dissatisfaction and how things could be different, was the growth of civil actions taken against the police outside of the complaints system. A growing number of complainants were successful in pursuing civil actions against police officers for malpractice whilst the complaints system apparently exonerated them. The situation was exacerbated by the fact that the Police Complaints Authority, and its predecessors, could find a complaint to be substantiated whilst at the same time no action was taken against any officer. In addition officers became very adept at using the system to their best advantage in terms of delay and procrastination, and then manipulating the medical retirement provisions to avoid any disciplinary hearing at all and retire on generous index-linked pensions.

The way in which this manipulation of the discipline system undermined public confidence in the police generally was obvious to all, yet senior management in the police service resisted any change. They were adamant that anything other than the criminal burden of proof exposed police officers to the unacceptable danger of false allegations being made and presumably proved. In this the Association of Chief Police Officers (ACPO) put its loyalty to police officers above its responsibility to the public. Any employee might find themselves open to false or malicious allegations. It did not appear to present insuperable difficulties to other enforcement agencies such as customs officers. Employment is a civil issue and should be judged on a civil standard of proof, i.e. the balance of probabilities. If ordinary employment law had been introduced to the police service in the early 1980s, it is highly probable that much of the damaging publicity which the service received, through officers both avoiding the discipline system and benefiting from generous pensions, may have been avoided and the current proposal to set up an independent investigative agency may have been unnecessary. It is not clear that the recent changes, introducing the civil standard for the burden of proof and the concept of dismissal for poor performance, will be as effective as they could be as the home secretary has been persuaded to complicate the test of proof with conditions that appear to move it to somewhere between the civil and the criminal one. Although the regulations state that the burden of proof is the balance of probabilities the guidance notes that the more serious cases, which will have a more serious outcome if proved, will need more persuasive evidence to merit a finding. This is perhaps a statement of the obvious, murder requires more weight of evidence than speeding, but the introduction of the condition was unnecessary and will now require legal interpretation to determine its significance. The Police Federation campaigned long and hard to retain a special position for police officers. While it is accepted that they are particularly susceptible to vexatious and malicious complaints, this in itself does not justify the new burden of proof which is likely to bring more satisfaction to lawyers than to the public.

The loss of confidence

Throughout the time covered there was a gradual bleeding away of confidence in the service through a number of factors. The first was a growing lack of confidence in police integrity as the list of corruption cases, in which the evidence was seen to be suspect, grew. This was occurring in the courts at every level but especially in the Court of Appeal. Many of these cases originated in the 1970s but it was impossible to manage the public debate to show that they reflected past and not current practice. This factor was compounded by the service's failure to deal with the enormous changes required in police practice through the Police and Criminal Evidence Act as already discussed.

The initial hopes raised in the black and Asian communities by the Scarman Inquiry were gradually whittled away by the fact that there was no obvious change in police practice, or more especially in the numbers of black and Asian police officers. The service response to this latter factor was to complain that not enough candidates came forward. As will be discussed in more detail later, the service did not see that it had a responsibility to ensure that this factor changed. This was compounded by the way in which inner city disturbances became associated in both the police and the political debate with criminality rather than discrimination and social deprivation.

Another factor was the relentless rise of crime which had been growing at a fairly steady rate in the late 1950s and 1960s and, as we have noted, increased significantly throughout the 1980s. An important factor in the internal police debate was how readily the service was willing to adopt the approach which stated that crime was everybody's responsibility and that the police could necessarily only play a fairly minor role. There was a growing culture of acceptance and tolerance of growing crime rates, which was not reversed until the early 1990s, in which the police were willing to blame other major factors for the growth without accepting their responsibility for performing better within the area that was their remit, i.e. the prevention and detection of those crimes which were amenable to positive police action. That said, it must always be borne in mind that confidence in the police by the general public has always been high. The loss of confidence was reflected in moving policing into the top five occupations rather than the top two or three: a position to which it has now returned.

Politicisation

The political situation in Britain in the 1980s was a very unusual one. The British political system is based on an active and able opposition; like the legal system it is critically dependent on confrontation and debate. In the 1980s there was effectively no opposition to the Conservative Party, other than within its own ranks. The 'left' was divided into three. The Labour Party, which had the largest numerical support, had moved to such an untenable position on the left that its 1983 Manifesto was described by Gerald Kaufman as 'the longest suicide note in history'. The newly formed Social Democratic Party (SDP) had come from the centre and right of the Labour Party and, some would argue, had robbed it of a significant part of its intellectual strength. Initially it generated an enthusiastic welcome from people who had, up until that time, not been involved in politics. As the decade developed however its support decreased and it eventually merged with the Liberal Party. As support for the Labour Party diminished, that for the Liberal Party increased, although the rate of increase was significantly affected by the creation of the SDP. All of this coming and going in the opposition meant that the Conservative Party had a fairly free hand in what it did, and a victory in the Falklands war, coupled with an economy improving after the deep recession of the early 1980s, led to a situation where the Conservatives could claim, with some confidence, to be the 'natural' party of government in the United Kingdom.

Police work by its very nature appears to attract to its ranks people who are conservative by nature and Conservative by politics. Anyone who doubts this has only to go into any police canteen, attend any police training course or sit in a transit van with 10 or 12 other police officers and listen to the conversation. If empirical proof is thought necessary then all that needs to be done is to look at the newspapers which they read. It will be found that the vast majority read, depending on the degree of intellectual stimulation they seek, the *Sun*, the *Daily Mail* or the *Daily Telegraph*. To be a *Mirror* reader is unusual and a *Guardian* reader is almost a term of abuse. Many senior officers will make much of the fact that they are politically impartial. Some, like Sir Robert Mark will say that they carry this to the point where they do not even vote. To do this is to confuse a mechanical exercise with thought. If one's intellect and reasoning leads one to support a certain political viewpoint, the exercise or not of the right to vote is irrelevant other than that it is a failure to carry out one's responsibility as a subject (as long as there is a monarchy this is the correct term). It is impossible to be politically impartial in thought, the key is to ensure that those thoughts are not reflected in operational decisions. That said, up until the 1980s the police service had an enviable reputation for carrying out its responsibilities with an impartiality which was unusual, even in the developed west.

In the 1980s the perception grew that the police were no longer impartial but actively supported the political stance being taken by the Conservative Party. There is little doubt that the key operational decisions which led to this lay around the handling of the miners' strike. In the 1970s it was clear that the police had been out-manoeuvred and out-thought by the striking miners. The enforced closure of the Shotley depot by Arthur Scargill's flying pickets still rankled. The government was determined that this would not happen again. That determination was shared, for different reasons, by the police. The government gave clear leadership. It was clear that resources would not be an issue and the police responded with a nationally organised campaign the like of which had never been seen before.

Police action in the Nottingham area was clearly warranted. The miners there had not elected to strike and there was a clear attempt to force them to do so by the flying pickets tactic which had worked so well in the 1970s. These miners had a right to be able to go to work and the police had a responsibility to ensure that they could carry out that right. However, there is no doubt that police tactics went beyond this proper exercise of power. To set up roadblocks half a mile from a pit could be argued relatively easily as operationally necessary. To set them up 10 miles from a pit is more difficult to justify but still possible. To set them up 150 miles from a pit, as happened at the Dartford Tunnel, was a clear abuse of power, regardless of the fact that it received some judicial support. In situations of conflict the key police role is to try to achieve a balance of rights and a decision of this nature could not be argued as balancing the rights of free movement and demonstration as at least equal to those of the miners who wished to go to work. In the same way it is clear that arrest and bail was used as a weapon of control. Again the judiciary played a role in this which will be dealt with later. It is clear from the ratio of arrests to prosecutions that this tactic was used by the police in order to gradually deplete the number of pickets. The most obviously disproportionate decision was that which created the situation of 1,000 police officers escorting one miner back to work. No matter how it is dressed up, this looks like a political decision and made the police look triumphalist.

The final factor which showed how the police as a body were moving and thinking was the decision of the Police Federation to invite a Conservative member of Parliament to be their representative in Parliament. The traditional position had been that the Federation representative was always a member of the opposition, usually a distinguished one. Whilst the Federation could argue that the Labour Party was now so far left and so disorganised and that it would have been inappropriate for them to select from that party, they could still have invited a member of the SDP or Liberal Party to take on the job. The decision to invite a Conservative MP to do it was an implicit endorsement of the 'natural government' claim of the Conservatives.

The 1990s: External and Internal Reform

As the service entered the decade it became aware, and was made aware, of the fact that it was seen to be failing in a number of areas, most notably the control of crime. In the period between 1989 and 1992, property crime exploded, increasing across the country by between 25 and 35 per cent. The police response was twofold; firstly, prompted by Michael Hirst, the then chief constable of Leicestershire, it began to seriously examine how the quality of service delivery could be improved. Secondly, it stated that it had not been given adequate direction by either the public or the government on what its priorities should be, arguing that the spectrum of activities in which the police are engaged inevitably mean that resources are too thinly spread. Greater focus was required and both government and the public were invited to provide it.

Both of these issues are in fact interrelated. The element which underpinned them, as discussed earlier, was the service's inability to adequately analyse problems; determine on an empirical basis what could be done;

recognise what the service was capable of achieving and what could only be achieved either by others or in conjunction with others; and from that develop effective action plans which could be monitored and reviewed. Much was made of the allegedly confused nature of the demands made by the public on the police. That contention was spurious. When the public were faced with the question of what they wanted done in the context of limited resources, i.e. when they were forced to identify priorities, it was found (in the Operational Police Review conducted by the police staff associations) that their priorities were almost identical to those of police officers. This meant that if the police service identified its priorities, publicised them and stated how it intended to improve the situation, it was highly probable that it would get public support for them. The difficulty faced by the police is the same as that facing any public body which has limitless demand but limited resources: while the mass can agree to the priorities, the individual wants their immediate need to be satisfied even where that need is outside of the agreed priorities. Where it is impossible to satisfy that immediate need, the service must learn how to shape expectation, both generally through public education, and specifically by dealing sympathetically with the individual describing what can, and cannot, be done.

External reform

The government meanwhile was becoming impatient with failure. It recognised that it had treated the police as a special case for over a decade and, now that the trade union issue was more or less settled, it was no longer dependent on the police to move its political agenda forward. In fact the agenda had moved from the politics of trade union control and the economy on to law and order and the police. The failure of the service to provide government with any assurance that it would affect crime in a positive way led to two major reforms: one of which was implemented fully, the other of which was poorly thought through and was deservedly undermined by the resistance of the Police Federation, leading to only partial implementation.

The first major change came in the Police and Magistrates Courts Act 1994. This gave the home secretary significantly new powers over both chief constables and police authorities and it redefined the tri-partite relationship between chief constables, police authorities and the Home Office. In essence it gave the Home Secretary the power to set objectives and directions for the service and it required that the chief constables devise and implement policing plans for the police authority for their area. It was the beginning of a significant trend of change in the relationships between the three elements of the tri-partite arrangement, a change which is still underway. In terms of the home secretary, it reflected the trend elsewhere for the powers of local government to be diminished in favour of central government. The detailed effects of this change will be dealt with in Chapter 7.

The second change was the Sheehy inquiry into police pay and conditions of service. This began with the 'bang' of proposals advocating fixed term contracts for all police officers, significant reductions in the rank structure, considerations on direct entry, single line budgets for chief constables, performance related pay and the removal of the housing allowance, all in the context of a debate which was highly critical of the service and its ability both to manage change and to deliver improved performance. It ended with the whimper of fixed term appointments for chief officers only, the removal of the ranks of deputy chief constable and chief superintendent. It left a totally confused picture for the rank of chief inspector and succeeded in removing the housing allowance. All of these 'improvements' have been criticised since their implementation and only those of fixed term appointments for chief officers and housing allowances remain, with a significant body of opinion calling for the restoration of the latter in order to balance the pay and conditions in the southeast of England in relation to the rest of the country. The only 'successful' recommendation, concerning fixed term appointments for chief officers, has also brought with it the disadvantage of discouraging some officers, relatively young in service, from coming forward for promotion to chief officer ranks until they can be sure that they will reach pensionable service before the end of the term.

In 1997 there was the first change of government for 18 years and it was clear that the new home secretary had not been sitting on his hands whilst in opposition. His first major piece of legislation was the Crime and Disorder Act 1998. This Act went some way towards implementing the recommendations of the Morgan Commission in that it created a statutory responsibility for crime prevention and reduction for county, district and unitary authorities (it also included the NHS but experience of the first three years showed that this inclusion has been notional rather than substantive). A significant feature from the police constitutional perspective was the fact that it made the chief constable and not the police authority a 'responsible authority' under the Act. The Act not only gave a statutory responsibility to these bodies but it also made them accountable in their performance to the home secretary, another small step towards centralised direction. It instituted a radical change in the way that youth offenders would be dealt with so as to enforce interagency co-operation. The effects of this latter change are still being developed, especially around the concept of pooled budgets rather than contributions in kind. It was a major plank in the Home Office's attempt to create 'joined-up' government but, after an initial wave of enthusiasm, it is still not clear that the local authorities have been willing or able to find the resources necessary to achieve real change outside of the youth offending provisions.

The second major change was the introduction of the concept of Best Value. This replaced Compulsory Competitive Tendering (CCT) which had been introduced by the Conservatives in order to contract out much of the servicing aspects of public service organisations e.g. vehicle fleet management, canteens, cleaning. CCT had been successful in focusing the public sector on the issue of costs and had achieved significant cost reductions. However it was accepted that the concept had gone as far as it could and in some areas, such as cleaning, was actually counter-productive in terms of quality and because of the burden of contract management. (The NHS is now attempting to reverse the worst aspects of this through ring-fenced funding and the return of matrons with specific responsibility to improve cleanliness in hospitals.) The idea of extending it to those services closer to 'core' functions e.g. research and planning, personnel management, had been resisted in the main and appeared to have been quietly abandoned by government. Best Value is a far more pervasive concept and was initially treated by most organisations with enthusiasm. Unfortunately the bureaucracy which grew up to accompany it has done much to undermine that initial enthusiasm. It has been described by CIPFA, the public accountants organisation not renowned for seeking out political controversy, as an 'excellent concept' converted into a 'bureaucratic nightmare'. However, there is no doubt that it will have a significant effect on how local and central government organisations both deliver service and organise themselves in the future. The constitutional difficulty in policing is that the police authority has the statutory responsibility for Best Value. The concept encompasses the whole of service delivery and must necessarily include operational issues. The constitutional position of the chief constable is that they are responsible for operational decisions. Again this will be dealt with at some length in Chapter 7. At the time of writing it has had little effect on the relationships between police authorities and their chief constables. It has the potential for significant confusion and disagreement.

A significant external factor in reform was the growing role of the HMIC and the Audit Commission. The former had a long established role in the inspection of police forces but its methodology changed quite profoundly in the 1990s to look at what was being achieved by way of outputs and outcomes rather than the traditional approach of examining inputs and policies. Some of this change was a result of the way in which the Audit Commission had developed its role, moving from traditional audit functions such as the examination of financial systems, through to the detailed examination of operational policing, beginning with the use of fingerprints and moving through eventually to the function and effectiveness of patrol. Theoretically, the Audit Commission developed inspection models which the HMIC used; in fact there has developed a considerable overlap which has yet to be satisfactorily resolved. By the end of the decade the service could fairly claim to be the most inspected element of government, with forces inspected annually by both HMIC and District Audit, whilst at the same time HMIC would carry out between three and six 'themed' inspections of issues such as diversity, police use of firearms etc.

Internal reform

The service made considerable progress during this time. Throughout the decade its ability to manage and improve performance became noticeably better. In the run-up to the elections in 1997 both political parties declared support for the police but both, in reality, reduced resources. There was an explosion in property crime between 1989 and 1992 when it grew by over 30 per cent. It continued to grow, although more slowly until 1995, since when there has been more or less continuous reductions. The situation initially benefited from demographic trends but the downward trend continued, especially in burglary, when these demographic factors became less favourable. This crime was a focus of government concern and as well as tasking the service to reduce it, changes were made in penal policy which most police officers would say had an effect on some career criminals who tended to switch from burglary to other forms of property crime, especially credit card fraud, where the probability of detection was relatively low and the penalty on conviction significantly less than that for burglary.

As the decade developed the service became more effective in managing resources and in developing a more 'intelligence-led' approach to both crime and to community problems. It is probably no coincidence that these changes occurred at the same time as the replacement of 'barons, bobbies and bosses' described by Robert Reiner (1991) with what he described as bureaucrats, i.e. scientific managers. There is no doubt that this trend is still underway and has some considerable way to go before the service can be confident that senior managers are comfortable with modern performance management techniques.

Early in the decade some forces had made steps to reduce overhead costs, especially management on-costs. After the Sheehy report all forces were directed to ensure that management costs were reduced. There is no doubt that the rank which bore the brunt of this pressure was that of superintendent both in terms of a significant reduction in overall numbers, and in a simplification of a rank structure, removing that of chief superintendent.

While this showed that the service could respond fairly quickly to pressures to change, the way that it was done reflected very badly on national cohesion with every force developing its own criteria for the changed rank structure and pay scales. This led in turn to the superintendents quite properly demanding that the same job should attract the same rates of pay and conditions of service everywhere in the country. The resulting drawn out negotiations effectively led to the reintroduction of the chief superintendent rank. From a service perspective this outcome seemed inevitable given the rather chaotic way in which the changes were introduced through the police negotiating process (an arcane and confused morass worthy of a book in itself). From a government perspective however it must have looked as if ACPO was incapable of developing a coherent national approach.

A significant feature of the early part of the decade was the attempt by the government to hive off police functions to other organisations where they could be done, if not better, then at least more cheaply. The vehicle tasked to achieve this was the Home Office Review of Core and Ancillary Tasks which was asked to examine all aspects of police work in order to identify what could be removed from the police remit, which was believed to be very expensive, and given to other organisations in the public sector, privatised or given to completely new organisations. The committee sat for two years and its outcome demonstrates very effectively the highly complex nature of police work. On the face of it a number of functions look as if they can be removed from the police and given to other organisations, as to the layman they looked like discreet tasks, for example, missing persons and traffic policing. Missing persons are an excellent example of the complexity issue. There is often an assumption that if something is not done very well then it is because of incompetence on the part of the organisation tasked to carry out the function. It is rarely accepted that it is often not done very well because it is very difficult to do. People who go missing deliberately make a choice to sever all of the connections which would make detection relatively straightforward; they change their name, their work, their place of residence (often to a distant part of the country). In a country with no national identification system it then becomes very difficult to track them down. The complexity of the task is that a 'missing person' can very often be a number of other things, most of which are clearly a police responsibility e.g. a murder victim, a vulnerable person either through age or intellectual ability, a victim of abuse or a fraudster on the run. It thus becomes impossible to separate out a task which is in the main relatively routine, (most people return home within hours rather than days), from those which require professional judgement on what needs to be done.

There were four major achievements for the service in the 1990s . Firstly, it managed in the main to retain public confidence despite the problems created by the Metropolitan Police handling of both the murder investigation of Stephen Lawrence and its treatment of the calls for an inquiry, and the subsequent deservedly scathing criticisms of the Macpherson Inquiry; the reversal of a large number of terrorist and serious crime convictions; and the explosion of crime in the first two years already described. Police officers find it at best ironic, and at worst irritating and insulting, when politicians and commentators draw attention to the fact that confidence in the police has declined. What they universally fail to also point out is that the decline is from exceptionally high levels to merely high or very high levels, when the same opinion polls show that the level of public confidence in politicians and journalists is usually low or almost non-existent. The vast majority of the population have reasonably high levels of confidence in the service and the levels of confidence in the Asian community as a whole replicate those of the white community. Even in the Afro-Caribbean community, where confidence in the police is understandably lowest, over one third of the older age group (40 plus), routinely express confidence in the service. There has always been, and probably always will be, a lower level of confidence among young people of whatever colour and class. It is not clear that there has been a significantly higher rate of decline in confidence in these age groups or that the polling mechanisms are becoming more accurate and more group focused.

Secondly, it managed to persuade two governments that more was not necessarily better when it came to setting objectives and priorities. Both governments attempted to set a completely unachievable level of objectives for the service, mainly in response to political pressure. It was a considerable achievement for the service to persuade both that the NHS model, where there were at one point over 200 'priorities' or key indicators, was not a particularly successful one and that the term priority lost its meaning when it was describing factors in double figures. Thirdly, it coped with significant changes in the constitutional position of the traditional tri-partite arrangements. The reasons for this are complex and will be dealt with in Chapter 7 but the changing role of the Home Office and police authorities in relation to the traditional position of the chief constable were considerable and could have distracted police leadership from the task in hand. Finally, some 10-15 years after Home Office Circular 114/83 it has begun to put in place measurement and targeting systems which can give it a real handle on what works and what does not; it can begin to demonstrate what is or is not cost effective and can begin to make 'predictive' decisions on the use of resources, i.e. if their use is changed what the effects of that change will be.

Conclusion

The discussion above may appear to be overly critical of the police service but it must be remembered that its purpose is not to praise the service but rather to explore those features of the British police service which will inhibit it from retaining its position as one of the best police services in the world, a context in which the pace and nature of change will be greater than ever before. There is no doubt that the service has achieved much in the period discussed. It has managed to remain predominantly unarmed despite the existence of a serious terrorist threat and the increased use of firearms by criminals, especially in the drugs trade. It has retained public confidence of the white and Asian population although it faces a mountain of a task if it is to gain the same level of confidence with the Afro-Caribbean community. It has shown an ability to be innovative and self-critical. Unfortunately, much of the former has been critically dependent on individuals and when they have moved on their innovation and improvements have too often withered on the vine. It has remained close to its roots in the community despite the significant changes in structure and the creation of some very large police forces. It has moved through, and is moving through, significant changes in its political accountability and has always shown a desire to retain local rather than national accountability, and always ensured that governments of whatever ilk have left room in their grand strategies to ensure that local concerns are also catered for. It has dealt with a period of serious disorder where any other service would have resorted to extreme, if not fatal, force and has done so with a minimum loss of life and a minimum use of force. In dealing with serious crime, especially murder, it has remained at the leading edge in the use of forensic science e.g. the use of DNA, and has a reputation which is second to none for investigation of this type of crime. It has significantly improved its approach to vulnerable victims, especially women victims of rape and domestic violence and to gay men and lesbian women in general.

However, there are underlying weaknesses which have existed throughout the period examined and which show few signs of being overcome. The service is still slow to recognise the impact of change and to pre-empt it with internal changes or external lobbying. Innovation tends to be patchy and critically dependent on individuals. A classic example of this is the use of 'problem-solving policing'. About every three to five years somebody somewhere in the United Kingdom introduces this as an innovation. The concept was first discussed in England in 1983 where its efficacy and appropriateness were recognised, yet it is still not the pervasive model of policing in any one force never mind the service as a whole. Part of the culture of the police, i.e. the 'canteen' or street culture is phenomenally resistant to change. When these two factors are combined it is not too surprising to find that much of what is done now is similar to that which was done 10, 15 or even 20 years ago. No other organisation has been allowed to do this. Even where the need for change is recognised it is usually slow in its introduction and is done so usually in 43 different ways. The remainder of this book will discuss the future pressures on the service, the current constitutional and management problems and how the service can be re-shaped to cope better with them and thus deliver a better level of service to the public and retain the service's pre-eminence in the world.

Chapter 2: The Thin Blue Line

Patrol

In policing, patrol is where the tyre hits the road. It is the public face of policing and delivers most of the services that the public expect. It covers a vast range of complex functions, takes up between 60 and 70 per cent of the police budget, is staffed by the widest range of officers in terms of age, service, skills and general aptitude yet is generally spoken of by politicians and commentators in the most simplistic terms, usually that of the 'bobby on the beat'. As if this were not enough that function also acts as the main training ground for police officers and is the general reserve, both of which features add to the complexity and difficulty of managing it.

When the public see police officers they are generally doing relatively mundane tasks or nothing at all: they are 'just patrolling'. Because of this the complexity of the job which is carried out is usually missed and both inside and outside the service the patrol officer is often spoken of in disparaging terms e.g. PC Plod, 'woodentops' (old Met CID slang). Patrol is in fact responsible for carrying out all of the following functions:

- **Emergency Response.** Every 999 call received by police is responded to by patrol officers regardless of the complexity. (The only real exception is kidnapping and extortion but even here the initial response can be by patrol). These calls range from old ladies trying to reset their VCRs, through complex road traffic accidents which involve serious injury or fatalities, to initial response to very serious crime where the protection of the scene may be vital to enable the recovery of the forensic evidence which may be the key to successful resolution.
- **General Incident Response.** These make up the bulk of police work and again go from the mundane of a person locked out of their home or car, through to difficult domestic disputes with complex histories which require considerable effort on the part of a number of agencies if they are to be resolved successfully.
- **Crime Investigation.** As well as being the initial response to most allegations of crime, uniform patrol is also responsible for investigating

the majority of less serious crime. Most serious crime is investigated by the CID, often augmented by special squads working on particular crime e.g. robbery squads, burglary squads, autocrime squads; even where they exist the remainder of crime is investigated by patrol and when the special squads deem themselves to be too busy they will often refer their 'overload' back to patrol. It is significant that patrol has no ability to pass on its 'overload' to anyone else but must absorb and deal with whatever is relegated to it. The nature of shiftwork makes it difficult for patrol officers to investigate crime effectively. They cannot change their work hours to fit the investigation as can the CID and the specialist squads, and it is impossible for them to contact the public or other agencies for a significant part of their duty time e.g. night shift, the first part of early turn and the latter part of late turn.

- **Order Maintenance.** All response to disorder in the streets or other public places is dealt with by patrol. Its key function is to anticipate where this may happen and try to prevent it by way of targeted patrol. Where it occurs its function is to restore order as quickly as possible using minimum force. This is significantly more complex than it looks as it is often necessary for police to stand by and contain groups, suffering verbal and physical abuse in the process, because there are insufficient numbers of police officers to make arrests. It usually takes two or more police officers to arrest any seriously violent prisoner and they then must escort that prisoner back to the police station where it may take between two and four hours to complete the arrest and charge process. Since the introduction of the Police and Criminal Evidence Act 1985 they can no longer immediately return to the scene to assist their colleagues after delivering the prisoner to the custody centre. In addition the officers must make that fine judgement of whether arrests will help restore order or merely exacerbate the situation.

- **Pro-active Patrol.** An increasing number of forces have developed more effective systems of directed patrol aimed at either specific community problems or gathering intelligence. This is probably the hardest element of patrol to organise effectively for two reasons. Firstly, the patrol officer is always anxious to be able to respond to emergency calls and because of this will avoid mundane tasks which might take up time. This is so despite the fact that they could leave the mundane should the emergency warrant it. It is a deeply ingrained cultural feature that the service has failed to eradicate. This has always been the case but it is now reinforced by the fact that all forces have target response times and shifts are measured on their success in reaching the target. They are rarely measured on their ability to affect community problems and the old management maxim of 'what gets measured gets done' is as true here as anywhere else. Secondly, most community problems are long-term and require action by the police and other agencies. As already described, the nature of shiftwork makes it very difficult for officers to become meaningfully involved and usually leads to them doing their best to mitigate the problem on the day, their objective being to ensure that they are not called back to it on their shift.

On top of all this the patrol function carries out two other key tasks in policing; those of training and acting as a general reserve. All police officers spend their first two years on probation and attached to patrol. Their initial training is a mixture of full-time training at a regional training school and on-the-job training, working with a tutor constable. At the end of this period the officer is certified as fit for patrolling alone and is turned loose on the public. The tutor system is a very good one and where it is done well the probationer constable will have been exposed to a fairly large range of tasks. However, it is impossible to expose officers to everything in this time and it is highly probable that in their first months of patrol they will come across issues/incidents which are new to them and in which they are expected to use their training and initiative to best advantage. It must be remembered that the dispatcher in the control room has no knowledge of the experience of the officer being dispatched so it is possible for a relatively junior officer to be the initial response to a serious incident. Since very few supervising officers actually patrol and they spend the bulk of their time in the police station, the probationer will need to deal with the incident and decide whether or not to call for assistance from either other officers or from a sergeant or inspector. (The situation is exacerbated somewhat by the fact that patrol is usually the first posting on promotion for both of these ranks.)

It would be fair to say that an officer is unlikely to be fully competent until they have between three and four years service. During this time the officer will attend a large number of incidents and will have been exposed to fairly continuous training. In most forces two things happen at about this point in service. The officer decides to go for promotion or to specialise, with the more able succeeding, and there is generally a drift away by mature officers from the busier parts of the force to the quiet parts. This is usually done as a result of them choosing to live as far away from the busy areas as they can in order to reduce housing costs and improve the quality of life for themselves and their family. The unfortunate consequence of this is that in most forces the busier and more complex areas are policed by the least experienced officers with the highest rate of abstraction for training. Every so often a chief officer will make a decision to reverse this and post experienced officers back into the busier areas. The morale consequences are usually disastrous and inevitably lead to the more incompetent or least popular officers being selected to be posted back. The effort usually lasts for one to two years and then is allowed to quietly fade away. The most spectacular example of this was in the Metropolitan Police in the late 1990s but it is a problem for most forces and one for which there is no easy answer.

The final function for patrol is to act as a general reserve both for the force and for the service nationally. The force reserve acts in two ways. Firstly, where there is a need to bring a large number of officers together for whatever reason, e.g. a difficult football match or a murder inquiry which requires large house-to-house inquiries, those officers are taken from the patrol function, often at very short notice. Secondly, the patrol function is used as the reserve for shortages elsewhere e.g. in CID or where the divisional commander has decided that more effort is needed. The hard reality is that specialists usually do a job better than generalists and there is always a temptation in the police service when a problem reaches unaccept-able levels to 'form a squad'. The squad is inevitably taken mainly, if not totally, from patrol. In addition, where there are national issues, such as the miners' strike, these officers are also taken almost exclusively from the patrol function. When the latter occurs the officers taken are inevitably the more experienced ones as they have usually completed the necessary public order training. This of course means that those left are the least experienced, but the nature of the task that is to be carried out remains the same.

The Shift System

The shift system for the British police is based on a rotating shift, covering 24 hours a day. There are four shifts, one early, one late, one nights and one off. The shift will usually work seven days followed by two off, with a long break between early duty and nights, finishing Thursday afternoon and beginning Monday night. The rotating shift is probably the least effective way of staffing the 24-hour function for two reasons. Firstly, it requires that the staffing level be divided equally in four and can, in theory, mean that there are as many officers on duty at 4 p.m. as there are at 4 a.m.. The workload is profoundly different at these times but experience shows that temporary movements of officers from one shift to another are rarely successful and create significant morale problems for the officers moved. One way, sensible in theory, of matching resource to demand is to overlap officers from one shift into another. For example it is not necessary to have the whole shift on duty at 6 a.m. and some officers could be paraded at 8 a.m., which will mean that they can then assist the late turn which is always the busiest shift. This rarely works for any length of time for a variety of reasons; the managers do not overlap so the overlapping officers tend to be ignored by the managers of the oncoming shift; they are not known by the oncoming shift and so tend to get the 'rubbish' jobs and thus feel devalued; there are often not enough radios or vehicles for the (now expanded) shift; most police officers have at least some paperwork to do and they will often use the overlap time to do this rather than assist the new shift; human nature being what it is the early shift will tend to ensure that the more competent officers are paraded early and the least competent or popular do the overlap thus adding to the devaluing process for the overlap officers. All of these factors tend to mean that, even when instituted, the system does not last long.

Secondly, an essential skill in policing is noticing the difference and being curious as to why that difference has occurred e.g. why is a teenager driving an expensive car? What is a child of school age doing in a town centre in the middle of the school day? Why is someone appearing to be trying to avoid scrutiny? The ability to do this is significantly enhanced if the officer can have permanence of place and time as they build up a picture of what is normal and thus can more easily identify the difference. There is no doubt that the most cost-effective system is that of fixed shifts. This allows the police commander to vary the staffing to suit the needs of the time of the day and day of the week. Since the officer is patrolling the same time zone they can build up a better picture and can have ownership of long-term problems as they will usually occur during the same time periods. It is a system used by a large number of the larger US forces. Generally speaking their new recruit joins the nightshift and gradually progresses to the more socially acceptable ones with experience. The Police Federation are completely committed to the retention of the rotating shift and it would not be possible for any one divisional commander or even any one force to contemplate the development of a fixed shift system within the restrictions of the current negotiating process for pay and conditions of service.

Most forces experiment from time to time with different shift systems, the best-known is the Ottawa system named after the city in Canada where it was first developed. There are a large number of variations on that system. Most forces however in the end return to the nationally agreed system as there are usually dysfunctional elements in other shift systems which cannot be overcome easily. Most of the non-standard systems require that there are more shifts, Ottawa for example requires five shifts. This has two immediate consequences. Firstly, it requires additional supervisory officers as there are now five teams to lead and not four. Secondly, the number of patrol officers remains the same therefore the number per shift is reduced. This means that the shifts are reduced to critical levels much more easily than they are when divided in four. In reality it means that Ottawa and its variations can only work in large police divisions as the smaller stations are usually working at or near critical levels on a day-to-day basis. The major advantage gained by the Ottawa-style shift is that it allows the divisional commander to have additional staff on some days of the week, usually Friday and Saturday evening. Since they come as a unit, i.e. with their own management team, they tend not to suffer the disadvantages of the overlap system although even here there is a tendency to use the time to do paperwork, take off time due etc., rather than augment patrol.

The usual cycle of experimentation in police forces is that an Ottawa-style system is introduced in one station. Because it does provide a better quality of life for the patrol officer it usually then spreads to other stations which have staffing levels which can cope. There is then discontent in the other stations where the staffing levels are too low to allow the creation of a fifth shift. The officers in those stations then come up with some other variation e.g. 12 hour shifts and this alternative then spreads to other smaller stations. Eventually it starts to become difficult to move officers from one station to another on a permanent or temporary basis because of the difference in shift systems and a decision is made to have a standard system for the whole force. Since any shift system other than the nationally agreed one can only be introduced if agreed by ballot, this almost inevitably means that the force returns to the national system and so the cycle begins again.

There is a real and urgent need to address this problem as its resolution is at the core of significantly improving the service delivered. It is inevitable that the patrol function will be seen to be the 'bottom of the heap' as far as status in the organisation is concerned. The way that recruits are introduced in the service means that it will always have a large training function and will always be staffed by significantly large numbers of relatively low-skilled and short-in-service officers. Its role as a general reserve means that the more able officers are taken away either permanently or occasionally in order to carry out other functions, with, from the patrol officer's perspective at least, no apparent thought as to the consequences that this has on the work of the shift. Status in any organisation is critically dependent on having something 'better' than others. That can be either money, attributes such as parking places or the ability to control one's own time and work rate. Most of these cannot be made available to patrol: but money can. There can be very few organisations in which significantly adverse conditions of service are not reflected in pay, yet this is the case in the police. The current situation is that the service has the least effective system, staffed by the least skilled and where police leaders are deprived of the ability to either introduce a more effective shift system or reward those who have the poorest conditions of service.

At present the shift system is negotiated nationally and can only be changed at force level with the agreement of the majority of officers, decided usually by ballot. This means that a workforce, which has secure employment for life, as a police force cannot go bust and police officers cannot be made redundant, must be persuaded to change and this can only be done by having something in the package which they find attractive. It is not surprising in these circumstances to find that the balance of advantage is usually to the officer rather than the force (and by logical extension the general public). When all of the above factors are considered, (particularly the fact that patrol takes up 60–70 per cent of the budget) it can be forcibly argued that police managers are asked to improve performance with one hand tied behind their back. Experience dictates that the Police Federation will not consider the introduction of fixed shifts nor an agreement whereby shifts can be introduced by the management decision of an individual force. Nor are they apparently willing to consider shift allowances which would enable management to compensate officers for working fixed shifts or the more inconvenient shift patterns and thus allow those officers working anti-social shifts to earn more than those who do not. Until this nettle is grasped it is difficult to see how the efficiency of the patrol function can be maximised.

Patrol Structure

Basically, patrol is structured around the twin axes of time and geography. The style of policing is often dictated by which of these factors is given pre-eminence. In terms of policing the rural areas there is very little difference between the ways that forces organise. The preferred model is usually based on teams of between 20 and 40 based on a small town and under the command of an inspector. The combination of a relatively small number of officers based on a manageable geographic area tends to mean that the officers build up a good picture of their area, they become known to key members of the community and the workload is such that they are usually able to deal with both the demand and the pro-active functions of patrol. This model usually only presents difficulties when budgets are tight and police numbers are reduced. Generally speaking teams of less than 25 to 30 have difficulty in providing 24-hour cover. When forces are faced with a reduction in budgets this leads to reductions in numbers of police. There is then a tendency to close the rural police station, withdraw these teams completely from rural areas and rely solely on mobile patrol based in the larger towns.

The real debate on policing models centres on urban policing. Most large towns have one or two large stations where police officers are based. In terms of cost efficiency this is sensible. The large stations can deal with all of the support systems required by the officer in terms of a public reporting point, a custody facility, a large multi-skilled CID, an intelligence cell and comprehensive administrative support. They will usually contain 2–300 police officers and anywhere between 50 and 150 civil staff, depending on how the administrative functions in the force are organised. From a structural perspective they are cost efficient. However, the combination of the large number of officers, along with, usually, a central location for the station, creates relative anonymity for the officers and a feeling by the community in the suburbs that they are neglected and are only really offered 'fire-brigade' policing.

When the function was based on foot patrol the solution was to create outlying stations where the officers were based. These would usually be strategically placed to maximise the area which could be covered by foot patrol: the area being divided into beats, each allocated a patrol officer. The change to vehicle-based patrol has made the issue more complicated and most forces have a time based team supplemented by officers dedicated to a particular area usually called something like Home Beat or Permanent Beat officers or more recently Beat Managers. A number of forces have tried to develop a more geographically based form of policing, most notably Surrey and the Metropolitan Police. The theory behind this is that the police area is sub-divided into a number of sectors, each policed by a small team, usually led by an inspector. This team then has ownership of the sector; can be held accountable for dealing with the more endemic problems; get a real benefit from developing a working relationship with the community; and is in turn 'owned' by its community.

While the concept works very well in a rural environment it does not transfer easily to an urban one where the time-based shift appears to exert an overwhelming gravitational force on the structure. While management believe that the teams are organised on a geographical basis, the officers know that the reality is that they are time-based teams with a more specific geographic allocation. The gravitational pull of the time-based team cannot be overstated. Police officers like to work in teams and the time-based team provides both a work and social context that reinforces this. Those forces that try to introduce geographic teams into urban environments find that they have to exert significant management effort continuously to maintain the structure of the geographic team. Like everything else management effort is a scarce resource and the question must be asked 'does the return on effort warrant this approach?' In terms of the outcomes there does not appear to be any measurable difference in performance between the approaches.

Visibility as A Measure of Effectiveness

There is no doubt that when the public respond to the question 'what additional security would you like provided?' they call for more visible uniform policing. In the last 20 or 30 years this has been reinforced by two other factors. Firstly, politicians have found it attractive to sell security by way of promising additional beat officers as it is an easy 'soundbite'. Secondly, chief constables have used the same argument to increase police resources generally because they are aware of how easy it is to sell to their authorities, this being so even when it was obvious to them that a better policing service could be delivered by investment in other things such as ICT. There was a brief moment in the 1990s when shrinking resources led both chief constables and the more enlightened politicians to look at the delivery of policing services in the round. That consensus has apparently disappeared and politicians are again engaged in something akin to medieval oath swearing, each promising to match or top the number of uniform patrol officers promised by the other.

There is ample evidence to show that whilst a uniformed police presence does not prevent crime as such, it does significantly reduce the amount of the sub-criminal anti-social behaviour and significantly reduces the fear of crime in the area patrolled (Wilson and Kelland, 1982). The 'broken window' theory of neighbourhood degeneration is now widely accepted and there is no doubt that a visible police presence has a significant impact on either reducing the rate of degradation or even reversing it. Since the approach works and it is quite clearly what the general public and their representatives want, why do the police not do more of it? Simply put they do not do it because other pressures direct their attention to other activities. From an external point of view there is a need to quickly service all emergency calls as the force and the shift are measured on this. In addition, the growth of proactive policing and directed patrol aimed at crime intelligence always gives the patrol officers something more attractive to do with their time. On top of this most patrol officers also have a caseload of crime to be investigated. Given the number of functions which the shift is expected to carry out, it is not surprising to find that officers give little value to an activity:

- Which has no visible return from their perspective.
- Where the benefits will be long-term at best.
- For which they will get little or no personal recognition by either their colleagues, their superiors or the public generally.
- Which if they try to pursue at the expense of refusing to take 'jobs' (dispatches from the control/information room), they are likely to be labelled as lazy or shirkers.

It is clear that if 'visibility' is to become an output of police effectiveness which is valued for itself rather than an input which contributes to other activities, there will need to be a significant increase in the overall numbers of police officers dedicated to patrol to achieve a noticeable difference in their visibility, especially if that visibility is associated with foot rather than car patrol. The Audit Commission study on patrol concluded that as little as five per cent of the overall patrol strength was actually on duty at any one time in urban areas. This simplistic, if not simple-minded use of statistics is a burden the service has to bear here and elsewhere. Since only 25 per cent of the total patrol strength is on duty at any one time (one shift) it is more accurate, and more reassuring to the public, to state that 20 per cent of the officers available are on patrol at any one time. It requires six to eight officers to staff a police vehicle (or a foot beat) for 24 hours; if the time coverage is limited to 12 to 16 hours then this will require three or four officers. A guesstimate to achieve a significantly improved police visibility in England and Wales would require 20–30,000 additional patrol officers. At the time of writing this would require about £500–750 million of additional expenditure. It is unlikely that any government would be willing to sustain this level of spending on the police service, especially if it could not guarantee that the additional officers would be used for the purpose of visibility and not other priorities identified by either chief officers or local shift commanders.

Basic Command Unit (BCU) and Shift Leadership

Another way to find the additional resources for patrol would be to make what is there more efficient and more effective. If patrol could be made 15–20 per cent more effective that would release for visibility something like the numbers and time described above. For example, the use of mobile data terminals in vehicles, if done imaginatively, could create 'mini police stations' where the officer could carry out a large number of administrative functions quicker and more efficiently, while still remaining 'visible'. The same tool would enable the sergeants and inspectors to manage the work of the shift from their vehicles, both providing extra visibility and closer support for the officers. In changes of this scale, the roles of the BCU commander and the shift commander are critical. The BCU is the core geographical unit in policing. It is usually either a large station serving a town or conurbation or is made up of a number of smaller stations. It has between 200–400 officers, serving a population of 150–250,000 people. The issue will be dealt with in more detail in the chapter on performance but there are a number of factors which must be dealt with briefly here. In my experience middle and junior police managers are highly effective crisis managers and competent in the running of their divisions or shifts on a day-to-day basis. However they are, with as always notable exceptions, poor strategic managers and poor change managers. It is difficult to decide whether or not this is a feature of the sort of person who joins the police (bearing in mind that everyone joins as a constable); a result of the police culture which is very much today and task centred; or if it is an outcome of the generally poor standard of police management training; or a combination of all of these factors. The failures described in Chapter 1 are those of ACPO. However the increase in resources at every level during the 1980s and early 1990s, coupled with the introduction at the same time in most forces of systems to reduce the paperwork burden on frontline policing through Administration Support Units and Crime Desks, appeared to lead only to a decrease in police performance.

This indicates that middle and junior managers were incapable of using the time released effectively but were content to allow the work to expand to fill the time available. A classic example of this is the double-crewing of vehicles. It is not rocket science to work out that single-crewing vehicles will mean twice the flexibility and visibility of double-crewing. Most, if not all, chief constables have a policy that vehicles should be single-crewed unless there are good operational reasons to the contrary. At their conference in 2000 the Superintendents' Association presented a number of proposals among which was that patrol cars should be single-crewed unless there were good operational reasons to double crew. Yet it is their members who run the BCUs where they routinely allow, condone or even encourage their own chief constable's policy on this to be flouted, usually because of pressures from patrol officers and their shift commanders.

In addition, the resistance to measurement of effort and results in these ranks was and is formidable. If one starts from the premise that a failure to measure and set targets is a willingness to live with failure then it is clear that these ranks, be it in their recruitment, selection or training, are in need of radical reform if the performance is to be significantly improved. The whole mess is compounded by what Waddington (1993) has described as the 'three-year rule': senior officers arrive, dismantle the initiative of their predecessors, introduce their own initiatives, and then leave before they have been fully implemented, allowing their successor to pronounce that their predecessor failed and repeat the cycle. It is unsurprising in these circumstances that junior officers tend to keep their heads down, knowing that the irritation will eventually go away and in the meantime they change the style and methods which they are used to by as little as possible.

Street Wardens

It is argued that a simple and straightforward solution to the visibility problem is the introduction of street wardens. That argument appears to have four premises:

- It is cheaper and thus more affordable.
- The street presence can be guaranteed.
- It is an acceptable alternative to the public.
- It can be as effective as a police presence.

Affordability

It is highly probable that street wardens would be provided by the private security industry and there is no doubt that the hourly wage cost of a security officer will always be lower than that of a police officer. There are however three factors which must be considered before concluding that this is all that there is to this part of the argument. Firstly, the advocates of warden systems usually accept that the public interest must be safeguarded by some sort of licensing or certification process. The main reason the security industry is able to offer such low rates of pay is that they generally employ people with lower skills and from whom very little is demanded. In order to gain the licence or certification it is likely that the staff will be required to be of previous good character and have a higher level of potential. It will be necessary to provide additional training to exploit that potential. It is inevitable that these factors will significantly raise the unit cost.

Secondly, the wardens will require an infrastructure. The current security industry is in the main static and has little in the way of a requirement for a sophisticated transport and communications infrastructure. Those which they have are relatively specialised, e.g. cash-in-transit. The need to provide this infrastructure will again add significantly to costs overall and will further reduce the cost margins between the security industry and the police, as every patrol officer currently added to the police establishment is achieved at little or no additional cost in this area. The final issue on costs is that police patrol, as discussed above, is provided by the lowest cost officers. The bulk of the patrol presence is provided by officers early in their service and at lowest rates of pay. The beat and patrol function is seen to be a training ground both for general policing and for the development of, or identification of aptitude for, specialist functions. Thus the real cost comparison between the patrol officer and the security officer is not the mid-point of the pay scale but one much lower down.

Street presence

There is no doubt that people recruited as street wardens would be limited to that task and their presence on the streets could be guaranteed as there would be no upward drift instigated by either them or their managers. In addition, as their function is essentially one of presence they would not be carrying out arrests or investigations which would necessarily remove them from public view. The same cannot be said of additional police officers. Apart from the duties which necessarily remove officers from patrol there are always a large number of specialist duties which could be better done if there were more resources available e.g. family protection, fraud squads, etc. There are thus always pressures on police managers to take people from patrol for these functions: the demand for the specialist service itself or the prompting by the officers to allow them to focus on more specialist and more satisfying work which has a higher status and which would assist them in either specialising or in gaining promotion.

Acceptability

Much of the support for a warden approach and for the expansion of the use of the private security industry is based on experience outside of the UK, especially that of the USA. It is submitted that this is a poor guide for a number of reasons. Firstly, the level of threat, especially to the person, is significantly different in the UK context when compared to its US counterpart. The level of threat in the US is such that it has created a pervasive armed security presence, even creating 'gated' communities which effectively keep the rest of the world at bay. This level of threat just does not exist in the UK nor are there any indicators that it is likely to in the foreseeable future. Secondly, the constitutional and legal approach to policing in the US is profoundly different from that of the UK. Although both are based on the common law, the political context has changed the way that law enforcement has developed in both countries. In the UK the process has been statute-driven, with the police having almost sole responsibility for police functions.

The US experience is very different. There are over 14,000 police forces there and they are complemented by a large number of national policing agencies. In addition there are a number of agencies and processes in the legal structure which include private individuals and companies, such as bail-bondsmen and bounty hunters. The situation differs further in the routine interchange which takes place between police forces and security organisations, in both personnel and constitutional terms. It is quite usual for police officers to work in their own time for private security companies, often using police issued equipment. (It must also be borne in mind in this context that police officers are almost always fully empowered regardless of their current task.) Indeed it is fairly common practice for police officers to carry out routine tasks for private companies, such as traffic direction at car parks during rush hours. These are not just built into police deployment practices but are an integral part of the process management uses to 'reward' officers through the chance to increase their earnings. It is not uncommon for small communities to set up their own police forces which they staff with officers from larger agencies working on their own time. On top of that are the 'gated' communities referred to above and the extensive use of armed security officers in shopping malls and industrial and trading estates. As a result of all this it is not surprising that the average member of the public is likely to accept interventions and directions from both police and security officers (the fact that both usually wear very similar uniforms and are visibly armed reinforces this).

In the UK on the other hand the security industry has always had a relatively low status and will normally expect any enforcement action to be done either by the police or with their support. It is unlikely that their mere creation and labelling as street wardens would significantly change this perception. There is even a danger that their ability to call on police resources will actually remove police presence from those areas which may deserve it more but lack the finances to afford wardens.

Effectiveness

It is generally accepted that the vast bulk of police work is encompassed by the description 'order maintenance'. People tend to call the police in those circumstances that involve 'something-that-ought-not-to-be-happening-and-about-which-someone-had-better-do-something-now!' (Bittner, 1975). Most of these encounters do not require the police to use force or carry out arrests but merely to restore calm, negotiate solutions and, most importantly, impose those solutions where necessary. All of the parties involved recognise the fact that the police officer has the real and immediate ability to carry out any threats of arrests or use of the criminal process. It is this real ability to impose order and solutions which allow the officer to be effective. The government has accepted the ACPO guidelines that the creation of a warden system should not also be accompanied by extending police powers to them. In these circumstances it seems as probable that the wardens will generate extra work for the police, calling them to trivial incidents which might otherwise be ignored, as they will reduce police workload.

Wardens cannot be introduced cost free. A warden scheme faces similar problems to the police in providing enough staff to make any noticeable difference in terms of visibility. The cost of doing so will be significant and the key question is whether or not it is 'Best Value' to spend on a concept which has no certainty of outcome, but which has predictable and perhaps insuperable weaknesses, rather than augmenting police forces so that they can better deal with endemic community problems and have the real ability to focus on visibility as a measured output, rather than as merely ancillary to other tasks which are deemed by the police, the public and government to be more important.

It is unlikely that there will ever again be the resources necessary to create the level of visibility which will be enough in itself to reduce the fear of crime. We will never again have a village or dedicated beat police officer. The answer to the problem lies in providing leadership at every level. At a national political level to engage in a mature debate on how the service should be properly resourced without tying it all simplistically to the numbers 'on the beat'. At local political level to use the framework that the Crime and Disorder Act 1998 has provided and really engage with police in providing effective inter-agency partnership: to focus on the end of removing problems completely rather than the means of suppression by the beat officer. At chief officer level to recognise the gains that can be made through more effective use of what is already there through more efficient shift systems and management. At superintendent level to use targets and measurement of community issues as a way of focusing patrol on these problems as well as emergency response and to recognise and applaud success in these areas at least as much as arrests for crime. At shift level to develop a more reflective management approach, taking control of what officers do rather than allowing them to set their own agenda. To do this it will be necessary to have clearly delineated action plans which integrate the work of all of the shifts and which have the potential to reduce or remove long term problems and which hold officers accountable. There are patches of good practice which show what can be done in most force areas: all that is required is that they become the norm rather than the exception.

Issues

The issues which arise from this description of the work of patrol are:

1. That patrol is the beating heart of the British police service and the success of the service stands or falls by the success of the patrol function.
2. Its resistance to change is demonstrated by how little the function has developed and changed since the introduction of car-based patrol.
3. Increasing its visibility is a proven way of reducing the fear of crime and it is worth the investment in time and resources needed to achieve this.

4. Uniform patrol is a highly effective system of order maintenance. The source of that effectiveness is the real ability to enforce order. Any warden or private security system which lacks police powers is unlikely to be as effective in either order maintenance or reducing the fear of crime.

5. It is possible to make patrol much more effective but only if there is a radical change in the shift system, a significant improvement in the service's ability to manage change and make the changes permanent, and a way is found to make patrol more attractive to experienced officers, much in the way that teaching is now being treated.

6. If patrol is to improve, middle and junior ranks must become more focused on improving performance over time, more reflective on what constitutes success in this function and less focused on merely managing the day-to-day function.

7. The difficulty in changing something as critical to improving performance as the shift system crystallises the problems that face chief constables in having to manage a local force using only nationally agreed pay and conditions.

Chapter 3: Diversity: Institutional White Male Chauvinism

The dictionary definition of diversity is 'being diverse; unlikeness; different kinds; variety; dissimilitude; heterogeneous; having unlike qualities.' In a police context it should mean that the service is representative of the community that it serves and should strive to reflect the different communities that it serves, having a broad spectrum of unlike qualities e.g. different religions, different religious and political views, a representative spread of age, gender and sexual orientation, race and disability, as far as that can be achieved. There are clearly levels of disability which would preclude police work and there are, for example, some religious groups whose unwillingness to accept the use of force in any circumstances would also preclude them. The key, however, is that the approach should be inclusionary to begin with and only exclude if there are good grounds to do so rather than exclusionary unless the applicant can establish grounds to be included.

The history of the service meant that to move from its 1970s profile to a completely representative force by the year 2000 would have been difficult under the best of circumstances. In the 1970s the service was predominantly white and male: this was further restricted in terms of physique, background and height (5' 8" was the minimum height for men and 5' 4" for women: a cause for ribald commentary on male Met. officers in the mid 1970s when an advertisement, trying to reassure women on equality of opportunity, said that the only difference was four inches). In addition, extensive recruitment from the cadet corps meant that a significant number of these white males had no experience of adult life outside of the police service. Women were tolerated rather than integrated, with forces having special women police units with a separate management structure. Women officers were focused on the 'female' issues of child protection and missing persons with a select few serving in mainstream policing, usually in specialist units such as drug squads where they were there as women rather than as detectives in their own right. In the 1970s the service could be fairly described as almost completely homogenous i.e. the opposite of diverse. Recruitment was done by interview and a character check. The inevitable 'cloning' effect that this would have reinforced this homogeneity. There were some black officers recruited at that time but these were very few with the majority of forces having no black officers at all. (The term 'black' is intended, throughout, to include all visible ethnic minorities unless otherwise stated.)

The political climate changed significantly in the 1970s with the introduction of sex discrimination legislation and the strengthening of the race discrimination legislation. Police forces reacted to the sex discrimination legislation by abolishing their specialist women's units, integrating women into mainstream policing. This removed the effective quota that had been placed on women's recruiting and the numbers increased, albeit slowly. The current situation is that women make up approximately 16.6 per cent of the current service, the vast majority of them being in the ranks of constable and sergeant with relatively poor representation in specialist units, especially those with a more 'macho' image such as firearms units, dog sections and special patrol groups (or their equivalent).

While there are now black officers in every force there are none in which the numbers are in any way representative and a figure of three to five per cent would be reckoned as being successful in current circumstances. In order to illustrate the scale of the task if the numbers are to be representative, I will use Bedfordshire as an example. There are currently 38 black officers. In order to be representative of the community there should be approximately 110–120. This would require a three-fold increase: and Bedfordshire has the fourth highest percentage in the country. The Home Secretary has set recruitment targets for all forces and while this is a significant step forward the questions raised are 'is the service, as currently structured and led, capable of change on this scale and is government able to sustain the political pressure required to achieve these targets through to the point where it is willing to invoke sanctions if it is not done?' In order to address the first part of this question, it will be useful to see how well or badly the service has managed to change concerning women officers who are the biggest visible minority within the service.

Gender Diversity

Following the introduction of the sex discrimination legislation forces gradually abolished their specialist women's units and moved women into front-line policing. There were two significant features of this change. Firstly, little thought was given to the work which the women officers did, especially in the area of child protection and, for a significant period of time, the gap was left largely unfilled as the patrol function was not capable of supporting it in the same way that the specialist units had done. The second feature was that the women were moved across into patrol with little or no training. This had a significant impact on sergeants and inspectors as they were expected to move into a totally different management structure, work 24-hour shifts (sometimes for the first time on a regular basis), and deal with operational issues which were new to them, with little in the way of training or support. This is not to say that this was a deliberate plan to undermine them or cause them to fail, but that it is characteristic of the way in which the service tends to ignore the cultural aspects and the complexity of a change of this nature. The ironic outcome of the change was that whereas with the specialist women's units women were represented at most ranks up to superintendent, on being integrated into mainstream policing, the senior ranks gradually fell away and women were only to be found in the junior ranks. By the mid 1980s very few forces had women superintendents and a significant number had none above the rank of inspector.

By the early 1990s the proportion of women in the service had increased slightly but their representation across it was still poor. There were very few in most forces above the rank of inspector and their representation in specialist units was either very low or non-existent. The introduction of equal opportunities legislation and policies should have changed this. While it has made a difference, it is still the case that women are significantly under-represented in senior ranks and in specialist units. By 2000, while 15 forces had women officers at ACPO rank, including three chief constables, 16 forces (37 per cent) had no women in the rank of superintendent, eight (18 per cent) had none in the rank of chief inspector, two had none in the rank of inspector and one force had no women at all above the rank of inspector. There are no nationally available figures to describe their distribution in terms of specialist units but it is unlikely that the situation here is any better and, given the cultural issues, it is highly probable that they are much worse.

The cultural resistance to women in the service cannot be overstated. In terms of equal opportunities the police service is lucky in terms of nomenclature in that 'police officer' is neutral. It is possible to use the same title without resorting to that level of political correctness that can cause so much amusement that it undermines the intention. Despite this there are still a significant number of forces which insist on using the term WPC rather than PC and the term policeman rather than police officer, a tendency perpetuated by the exclusive language used by the media. When this is done by senior management it is an implicit encouragement to those at every level to continue to use paternalistic and demeaning descriptions such as 'wobblies and woopsies'. Even in forces where the policy has changed and has been implemented fairly rigorously there are still a significant number of underhand tricks and devices employed to 'keep women in their place'. Examples of such devices are pressuring women officers during their probationary phase to wear skirts knowing that this will cause them difficulty or embarrassment in carrying out routine operational duties (this happens even where force policy clearly gives the woman freedom of choice); specialist units only stocking the larger sizes of protective clothing, boots and other specialist equipment so that the women feel stupid or uncomfortable when wearing them; using revolvers rather than semi-automatic pistols because of the difference in trigger pressure; introducing strength tests which are not connected to the job profile and which would ensure that the majority of women would fail, so that women who seek to join find it difficult if not impossible to carry out the tests. From the male officer perspective this is often described as being 'just a bit of fun'; but there is no doubt that it has an effect both on the women trying to go through the entry procedures and, more importantly, on ensuring that a large number do not come forward at all. Where they exist it is proof that the women do not feel able to raise the issues with senior officers as they cannot be sure how they will be received, or, even worse, that they are sure that the senior officers actively or tacitly support such practices.

In summary, the position in the police service some 25 years after the introduction of the initial sex discrimination legislation and after more than 10 years of equal opportunities legislation and policy development is that women make up less than 17 per cent of the service. They are still not well represented across the spectrum of police activity but tend to be restricted to either patrol or work such as family protection. They have a poor representation across the ranks, and the picture nationally is very patchy. This must be seen against the fact that, in my experience, women recruits are generally better qualified academically and have a more relevant employment background before joining the service. It cannot be argued that lack of talent and ability in women officers the cause of their relative sparsity in specialisms and in senior ranks. It can only be attributed to a deeply ingrained cultural resistance to their acceptance. A number of forces are tackling the issue robustly through the introduction of effective selective mechanisms that are based on competencies and evidence. However, the key issues are the snail's pace of progress which has been made in the time since 1975 and, even more disturbing, the very patchy performance that the service has achieved when examined nationally.

Race

So much for gender. What of race? The test of diversity here has been based on two issues; firstly, the ability of the service to recruit from the visible minority communities; secondly, its ability to deliver services and enforce the law in a way which is not only equal but is seen to be equal. The service delivery aspect will be dealt with later; here I will deal with the issue of recruitment. The Metropolitan Police recruited the first black officer in 1968. The event merited a lot of publicity at the time but little progress was made subsequently to increase the number of colleagues joining him.

Throughout the 1970s recruiting black officers was not seen to be a major priority and the numbers remained very low. In his report on the Brixton disorders in 1981, Lord Scarman recommended 'that the Home Office, with Chief Officers of Police, in consultation with Police Authorities and representatives of the ethnic minority communities, conduct an urgent study of ways of improving ethnic minority recruitment into the regular police and of involving ethnic minorities more in police-related activities'. Most forces, certainly those with significant ethnic minority populations, then put more effort into the recruitment of officers from the ethnic minorities. This was usually done through advertising campaigns and appeals to the leaders of the minority communities. The numbers increased, but only slightly, so that by the early 1990s most forces which had significant minority communities, had barely two to three per cent of their force recruited from these communities.

The numbers plateaued at this level and the usual response to complaints from the minority communities that the police were not representative was that the police had done everything they could but that not enough suitable candidates were willing to apply. Although the overall numbers were significantly smaller, as with women officers, the vast majority of these officers remained as constables or sergeants and were rarely found in specialist units. Some forces continued to try to develop more effective methods of involving the minority communities and of improving their recruiting profile. However this was made very difficult in the mid and late 1990s when the service was faced with budgets which did not cover inflation and which could only be met by reducing or even freezing recruitment. Clearly if a force is not recruiting at all it can do nothing to change its profile. This was certainly the situation faced in Bedfordshire. It was impossible to make commitments by way of recruiting campaigns involving minority communities, as it was impossible to say, year on year, whether or not any recruiting would take place at all.

In 1999 the service suffered the seismic shock of the report by Sir William Macpherson on the murder of Stephen Lawrence. From my perspective the three most significant outcomes of the inquiry were:

- Macpherson's recommendations dealt with the cultural issues as opposed to the process and structural issues that had been addressed by Scarman.
- Macpherson made it clear that the responsibility for changing things lay with those organisations with the power to do so, i.e. with the police and not with the community.
- The finding of 'institutional racism'.

Culture Versus Process

The Scarman report concentrated on the process of recruitment, training, the use of equipment and the mechanics of community involvement. Macpherson, on the other hand, accepted that the Metropolitan Police had adequate or good processes and policies in place, but recognised that they had not been followed in the investigation of the murder. The difference between Macpherson and Scarman is crystallised by the way in which they indicated what they wanted done. In his recommendations Scarman covered the whole gamut of policing, education, housing, employment and community involvement. In the main his is the language of exhortation in which he, 'concurred, agreed, endorsed, suggested, commended and called for' changes to be made. He made 15 recommendations, 12 of which applied to the police or changes in the law.

On the other hand Macpherson made 70 recommendations, only five of which applied to education, the rest gave a detailed prescription of what needed to be done. Critically, those issues such as recruiting, the exercise of powers to stop and search, strategies for the prevention, recording, investigation and prosecution of racist incidents, multi-agency co-operation and training are to be monitored in terms not just of their implementation but also of their effectiveness and in the outcomes obtained. The issue of managing police performance will be dealt with in detail in Chapter 6, the only point raised here is that meaningful targets are key to progress. Their absence shows that there is a lack of measurement and that success has not been described. If success has not been described then failure cannot be recognised, thus to fail to set targets and monitor performance against those targets is to accept failure. It is clear that Macpherson is not willing to live with that outcome; it is not yet clear whether or not the political will exists to ensure that his expectations are realised.

Responsibility

The second major difference concerns accountability for making things change. Scarman implicitly states that both the police and the ethnic minority communities share in the responsibility for moving the agenda forward. Macpherson makes it clear that it is the organisation or institution with the power to change things, which has total responsibility. It must take its audience as it finds it and if there is a lack of co-operation then it is its responsibility to find a way of changing that too. This means that there can be clarity of accountability and that chief officers can no longer pass the burden of responsibility back to the ethnic minority communities but must accept that if there is reluctance to join the police, be involved in community initiatives, to report racist attacks, then the responsibility for changing this paradigm lies with the chief officer, the police authority and the Home Office. This reflects a sea change in the way in which the police and other agencies should be held accountable in the future: if they find a reluctance to be involved on the part of the ethnic minority communities then the first stage of their action plan must be to find a way around that reluctance. They cannot use it as an excuse for taking no further action, as was the case pre-Macpherson.

Institutional Racism

The most difficult issue for the service to accept and move on following the Macpherson report was the allegation that it was 'institutionally racist'. A number of chief officers accepted this description in order to attempt to move the debate on from the past to the future, but not all did. The description was rejected forcibly by the Police Federation and, in those forces where the chief constable had agreed with the description, there was a universal feeling of betrayal by front-line police officers. I have no doubt that the description, as defined in the report, is a fair and accurate one of the service's attitude to race and, two years on, I believe that the description is accepted, with varying degrees of enthusiasm, by chief officers. Equally importantly it is accepted that it applies to most, if not all, government agencies, not least being the Home Office itself:

> . . . *the police service, in that respect (institutional racism), is little different from other parts of the criminal justice system: or from Government Departments, including the Home Office, and many other institutions.*
> (Home Secretary Mr Jack Straw, *Hansard* 24/2/99).

It has been accepted as applying to local government and the N.H.S. (the Chair of the Association of Local Government and the British Medical Association, *The Guardian* 24/2/99); The Royal College of Nursing (the Royal College Secretary, *The Guardian* 12/3/99); the legal profession (the Minority Lawyers Conference, *The Times* 16/3/99); and schools (Chris

Gould, OFSTED, *The Guardian* 11/3/99). It is accepted that it exists. What is not entirely clear is what is to be done about it.

The major difference that the use of the expression institutional racism made was that it finally ended the debate around the 'bad apple theory', i.e. that the situations and organisations are sound and that those instances of discrimination or improper behaviour are due to some misguided or poorly managed individuals. As long as the focus was on the individual it was unlikely that any real progress could be made. That said, the use of the term also creates some significant difficulties. The point is probably best made by Philips (quoted in Singh, 2000) who states:

> . . . *the concept (of institutional racism) is often used in a loose descriptive manner and has come to embrace a range of meanings, which are often imprecise, sometimes contradictory and frequently lacking theoretical rigour. Discussions of individual attitudes, stereotyping, implicit guidelines, explicit rules and procedures, organisational arrangements, power-sharing and struc-tural determinants of minority status have all been subsumed within the analysis of institutional racism.*

The problems are less when service delivery and law enforcement are considered, indeed it was in that context that Macpherson described it as:

> . . . *the collective failure of an organisation **to provide an appropriate and professional service** to people because of their colour, culture or ethnic origin. It can be seen or detected in processes, attitudes, and behaviour which amount to discrimination through unwitting prejudice, ignorance, thoughtlessness and racist stereotyping which disadvantage minority ethnic people.* (My emphasis).

In service delivery it is possible to look at outcomes which are in the main measurable and then realign policy and practice to ensure that inappropriate behaviour is corrected and that policies and procedures minimise or eliminate the probability of disadvantage or discrimination. Indeed the service is very good at this as its experience with the Audit Commission indicates. The service has shown itself to be so keen to implement changes recommended by the Commission, and thus avoid criticism, that the Commission has had to change its working methods when dealing with the police in order to stop the service acting too quickly whilst the Commission was still researching the issue and finalising its conclusions.

Recruitment (but not selection once recruited) presents a significantly different problem. It is best described as the difficulty in separating that disadvantage black people suffer:

- Due to institutional factors in policing.
- On a societal basis because they are black.
- Because of other factors such as class or gender.

As Singh (2000) states:

> . . . *writers have asserted that where ' black ' inequality exists so does institutional racism. However, 'black' disadvantage can accrue from a number of areas. 'Black' workers are still overwhelmingly represented in the working classes. Hence, 'black' people's experiences will be shaped by disadvantages that accrue from a class position. Similarly, 'black' women face the 'triple oppression' of class, gender, and racism. Class and gender, then, are both influential in shaping 'black' disadvantage. However, can we say that practices and policies that discriminate along the lines of class and gender are racist? If we follow the logic of institutional racism the answer is yes because these practices and policies help generate and reproduce 'black' inequality. Thus, in effect we have an inflated concept of institutional racism that has no discriminatory powers between the effects of racism and other social processes. This, in turn, weakens the analysis and suggests inappropriate policies that are designed to alleviate 'black disadvantage'.*

As if this were not enough, as our ethnically mixed society matures the definition of 'ethnic minority' becomes more and more obscure. Young black and Asian people, born and brought up in the UK, do not necessarily see themselves as disadvantaged to the extent that they merit any kind of special pleading or provision. They may even be offended by an approach that singles them out in this way. Their attitude to disadvantage may have more to do with class, education and family circumstance than race. This means that the service must continually check the validity of its assumptions, and their application to a particular target group, in trying to attract recruits.

Macpherson has made the police responsibility clear. It is the service's task to find a way around this difficulty but the size of the problem should not be underestimated. To use Bedfordshire as an example, even before Macpherson reported and his recommendations were known we had developed a strategy to improve recruitment that was wholeheartedly endorsed by Her Majesty's Chief Inspector of Constabulary. We had put together a coherent and co-ordinated system which:

- Linked in with the local ethnic minority community.
- Advertised extensively in the ethnic press.
- Gained publicity in that press for the successes of ethnic minority police officers in Bedfordshire.
- Had a system of follow-up with applicants to ensure that if they had any enthusiasm for the service as a career we could exploit it.

- Established a post with specific responsibility for maintaining contact with potential recruits from the minority communities.
- Ran familiarisation courses on both the police service and on the recruitment process (such is the scarcity of these courses that we attracted people from all over England).
- Included officers from the Black Police Officers Association in the selection process.

The whole system had a sophisticated monitoring and review mechanism so that we could identify areas of potential weakness and strength. Despite all of this we only increased our overall numbers by **one** in a year when recruiting generally was quite high. The major difficulties we face as a force are that we are an island of relatively good practice (percentages of black officers are: Bedfordshire 3.5, Hertfordshire 1.7, Cambridgeshire 2.6, Northamptonshire 2.6 and Thames Valley 2.4) and that our size relative to the Metropolitan Police made it very difficult to make any impression which was not quickly overwhelmed by what was going on in London at the time.

The home secretary has established an action programme to follow up on Macpherson's recommendations. This is an initiative which will help to ensure that they are not lost sight of or allowed to wither on the vine. In addition, the law on race has been amended to create a positive duty to establish sound race relations in public bodies. It is too early to say how effective these will be as forces are currently, in the main, establishing processes and procedures and are not able to report on outcomes. Their effectiveness will only be judged on whether or not they make a difference in terms of changing the profile of the service and guaranteeing equality of service delivery. The service's performance in dealing with equality of opportunity as far as women are concerned is not encouraging. The paradigm shift required to achieve a truly representative police service is massive. A survey of Metropolitan Police staff (unpublished) was reported by *The Observer*, 14th January 2001, to show that 56 per cent of staff believed that people are treated differently according to their ethnicity; five per cent witnessed racism often or sometimes; 36 per cent witnessed it at some time; and one per cent of officers still witness it in their units 'very often' (this is the equivalent of 260 officers).

The culture has shown itself to be highly resistant to change that it did not welcome and it is difficult to see how the shift can be achieved without significant differences also being made in the areas of sanctions and rewards, stability of management, improvements in change management, especially that involving cultural change, and how chief constables and police authorities are to be held accountable for changes in outcomes rather than the mere implementation of processes and procedures. Even with all of this, the survey carried out by *The Guardian*, 24th February 2001 showed that two years after Macpherson's recommendations the number of ethnic minority officers in England and Wales had only gone up by 154, with some forces actually going the wrong way. The major difficulty is visibly demonstrating to young black people that the service has equality of opportunity. This can only be done by having black people in senior posts. When this factor is taken together with the difficulty of changing the culture at street level, the question must be asked whether or not the recruiting process can stay as it is or whether the nettle of direct entry to senior ranks and specialisms must finally be grasped. At the current rate of progress it will take all of the 21st century for the service to become truly representative, too long for even the most supportive police apologist.

Sexual Orientation and Disability

The final two areas of diversity to be dealt with are those of gender-orientation and disability (the concept of a broad political spectrum in the police service is beyond even my creative thinking as that problem appears to be a universal one). Little is known about discrimination against gay men and lesbian women in the service as the hostility to them has been such that they have in the main remained 'in the closet'. I come to this conclusion as a result of having been involved in selection processes both within the forces that I have served with and at national level and have yet to come across a candidate who was openly gay. Having seen how the service has dealt with the issue of race and women this has probably been a sensible tactic on their part. However, it can be said with some confidence that if the service can develop a culture which can create true equality of opportunity in terms of race and gender, then it will probably be able to deal with this issue successfully.

The issue of disability creates a far greater challenge. The way that the service has dealt with women in particular, leaves the impression that 'the culture' appears to react in two ways, both of which will apply to any suggestion to include the disabled in mainstream policing. Firstly, by making a paternalistic judgement on what women should be allowed to do, either for their own good so as not to expose them to unacceptable (to their male colleagues) levels of danger; or that 'society' would not put up with it. Much the same debate is currently in progress regarding the use of women in the infantry. (It is ironic that at the same time that this debate was taking place a young woman came a very close second in the gruelling single-handed round-the-world non-stop yacht race.) The only acceptable test is, 'do women with the requisite skills, ability and commitment want to do the job?' This must be the test for everyone if equality of opportunity is to have any meaning.

The second reason is more pernicious; it appears to be based on the reasoning that if it can be shown that women can do the job then this in some way diminishes the value of the job itself, and thus the value of the male officer. On this hypothesis it can be seen that acknowledging that some aspects of the job can be done effectively by people with a disability will be extremely difficult. It is possible to point to some aspects of police work in general terms which can be carried out by people with disability e.g. call centres, some administrative tasks etc. However at best this is a fudge. It is possible to envisage certain police tasks that can be carried out effectively by people with disabilities, notably certain types of investigation such as fraud and in some roles in the intelligence function. Again, it would be a fudge to give such employees a more limited civilian role as police powers are often required in order to obtain judicial orders and to carry out certain tasks. It would be treating them like second-class citizens not to ensure that they had the police powers that they required to carry out their job effectively. In order to achieve this it would be necessary to abolish the single entry system. This also has its attractions for the reasons described above and later when the issue of police leadership is discussed.

Service Delivery

In theory this should not be too difficult for the service and as described above its record in implementing Audit Commission recommendations is probably the best in the public sector. The Metropolitan Police can be commended on the work that it has done in this area in the setting up of the Racial and Violent Crime Task Force under DAC John Grieve, increasing the number of racist incidents in terms of both reporting and detections and setting up the Advisory Panel. At a national level ACPO has developed, and forces have begun to implement, strategies to deal with hate crime and to ensure uniform levels of service from family liaison officers. Race awareness training is also being reviewed. However, it must not be assumed that the actions taken by the Met. and some other forces are necessarily reflected country-wide. Just as recruiting and selection are the litmus test of equality of opportunity, so the use of the powers to stop and search is the litmus test of attitude and service delivery to minority communities. Yet in HMIC's report, *Winning the Race; Embracing Diversity*, it is reported that in the key area of stop and search (and this is salutary in view of the way that gender diversity has been dealt with), HMIC identified, with some exceptions, continuing complacency amongst some forces on stop and search and ineffective supervision of the tactic and analysis of the data.

On race awareness training HMIC found an inconsistent picture across England and Wales with some forces having the key elements of training firmly in place while others *'had no such training'*, an indicator that some forces outside of London believe that Macpherson only applies to the Met. (Hadley, 1999). Again it is useful to look at what has happened, and is happening, to women to understand the scale of the task. The service has been exhorted for at least two decades to improve the way that it deals with domestic violence. The tactics and strategies that will be effective are well known and most have been empirically tried and tested. Most forces will have well written policies, but very few forces have introduced meaningful targets and are thus willing to live with failure. Processes and policies are not enough. It is essential that forces are judged by the outcomes they achieve and that there is clear accountability for those outcomes.

Issues

1. It is essential to recognise the scale of the problem and to appreciate that the change required in the cultural paradigm is at a level never achieved by the service.
2. Macpherson has described a useful set of performance indicators for the service but the key will be to monitor progress and hold chief constables and police authorities accountable for outcomes.
3. The way that the service has dealt with women, both as employees and as service recipients, indicates that progress will be slow and that change will be very patchy if viewed nationally.
4. The strength of cultural resistance is such that it will stop or even reverse unless it is kept under continuous review.
5. Almost nothing is known about the gay and lesbian experience in the service although the picture in service provision is changing, at least at policy level.
6. In order to change the profile of senior and specialist ranks to reassure the black community of real commitment to equality of opportunity and to include the disabled in policing it will be necessary to take a radical approach to the issue and consider direct entry into senior posts and specialisms.

Chapter 4: Policing Philosophy: Principle or Pragmatism?

The first question to be resolved is whether or not there is a philosophy or general principles of policing or whether there should be such general principles. It is important to separate principles of law by which the police are bound and general principles which underpin policing. For example the use of minimum force is a legal requirement under the common law and binds not only the police but also every citizen and even the armed forces when called in to aid the civil power. However, the commitment of the service to this when seen in the light of its reluctance to introduce more invasive forms of force such as extended batons and CS incapacitant, and its determination to remain unarmed, begins to look more like a general principle of policing. It is certainly an approach which is almost unique in the world. It is also difficult to tell where the philosophy which sustains government in general ends and that of an arm of its executive begins. In this context 'policing by consent' has little more meaning than 'educating by consent' or 'traffic direction by consent' – they are all part of the contract that the subject has with government.

There are very few philosophers who have written specifically on the issue of policing and very few police practitioners who have done so. The most notable is John Alderson, ex-chief constable of Devon and Cornwall. Alderson focuses on the 'high police command' and its responsibility to work in accordance with general philosophical principles. He comes to the conclusion that the general principles should be based on a contractual relationship between the subject and the government, in which the police perform the function of maximising freedoms while at the same time controlling disorder and preventing the state from slipping into anarchy. Achieving this balance, he accepted, calls for great skill and determination. The difficulty that his description gives a practitioner is that it is full of undefined terms which in the end are essentially value judgments such as 'harm' and 'common good'. Like the concept of 'reasonableness', these terms can only be interpreted in context. In policing terms that context will inevitably be complex with a large number of conflicting interests, all demanding supremacy.

More recently Peter Neyroud and others have very usefully gleaned eight general principles to be used by police officers to help provide answers to such dilemmas. They are:

- respect for personal autonomy
- beneficence
- non-maleficence
- justice
- responsibility
- care
- honesty
- stewardship

The difficulty I have with these principles is that they would appear to apply to any public office in which the office holder had both power and discretion. The particular office may emphasise some of these principles more than others but it is unlikely that they would not all apply. If that is the case, it is difficult to see what it is about the nature of policing which makes it different from these other public bodies. In addition both Neyroud and Alderson described their principles as the ideals to which a police service should subscribe. Neither states that they are principles which are currently universally applied.

It would clearly be useful, some may say essential (but if so, why has it taken so long to describe them), to have an agreed set of principles for the service, as they would be independent of time and could be used in both the training and operational context to ensure uniformity of treatment and decision-making over both time and geography. In order to establish what principles are applied by the service it is necessary to examine what it has done when working at the edge rather than what it does when working with the generality. The real test of whether or not principles apply is when they are applied regardless of outcome. Any organisation, institution or society which first looked to the outcome and then pursued it regardless of principle, is following at best a crude utilitarian approach, or at worst a despotic one.

In order to establish whether or not there are principles which have been applied over time, it will be useful to look at how the service has dealt with issues which it has seen as the key to its overall success and in which individuals have been presented with the very dilemmas described by

Neyroud. In order to do this I will look at issues which have spanned the decades and which in my view show a consistent approach. Those issues are; the Judges' Rules; the case of the Birmingham Six; the miners' strike; and the case of the Cardiff Three.

The Judges' Rules

These were rules which were developed by the judiciary in order to guide the police service on which methods were, and which were not, acceptable in questioning suspects in order to obtain confessions. In brief they required that the police were not oppressive, did not use inducements or tricks and, in essence, treated suspects fairly so that the confession could be seen to be truly voluntary. I doubt that there was a police officer in the land who thought that they were applied appropriately all the time or who did not know or suspect that in most serious cases they were substantially ignored. Since most judges in their careers acted for both the prosecution and the defence, it seems highly unlikely that they did not share these suspicions, if not this belief. Despite this, throughout the 1960s and 1970s confessional evidence was admitted either in the face of substantial evidence that it was obtained outside of the rules, or it was accepted that the rules had not been followed but that it should still be admitted.

Two principles appear to follow from this. Firstly, in pursuit of a conviction for whatever reason, and it is accepted that it was often based on a genuine belief by the investigator that the suspect was guilty, police officers were willing to ignore directions from the judiciary which were intended to ensure fair treatment of suspects, based solely on their belief of the suspect's guilt. Secondly, by giving the police such latitude the judiciary was giving the police service a clear, if implicit, direction that adherence to their rules was not always necessary if the greater good of society could be served by the conviction of the guilty.

The Birmingham Six

In brief, the Six were arrested immediately after the bombing of Birmingham city centre in November 1974. The forensic tests taken immediately following their arrests appeared to find traces of nitro-glycerine on two of them. They were interrogated over a period of four days during which some of them made confessions which implicated themselves and others. At the time of the arrests the pressure on West Midlands Police to make arrests was enormous and the speed of the arrests greatly reassured the public that the probability of further such attacks had been minimised or eliminated. At their trial they alleged that the confessions had been obtained as a result of either violence or the threat of violence and that the police officers' description of the interrogation process was a lie. They were convicted.

They continued to protest their innocence and attempted in 1977 to institute civil proceedings against the police for assault. The Court of Appeal rejected their case in 1988 where Lord Denning, the Master of the Rolls stated that:

> *If the six men win, it will mean that the police were guilty of perjury, that they were guilty of violence and threats, that the confessions were involuntary and were improperly admitted in evidence and that the convictions were erroneous. That would mean the Home Secretary would either have to recommend they may be pardoned or he would have to remit the case to the Court of Appeal. This is such an appalling vista that every sensible person in the land would say: it cannot be right these actions should go any further.*

He was later to say following the acquittal:

> *. . . if anything has gone wrong, it's the police, the West Midlands police, who are said to have been guilty of perjury. That's what's gone wrong, not our system of justice, it's the police.*
>
> (The *Guardian*, 15th March 1991)

In 1988 the Home Secretary was persuaded to refer the criminal case back to the Court of Appeal where the case again failed. There Lord Lane, the Lord Chief Justice stated: '*the longer this hearing has gone on, the more convinced this court has become that the verdict of the jury was correct*'. In 1991, only three years later, the case was referred back to the Court of Appeal where their appeals were allowed following the discrediting of the confessional and forensic evidence.

For the purpose of debate here I do not intend to discuss the original trial as it took place at a time when mainland Britain was under sustained attack from the Provisional IRA and when the rules of evidence had to be judged by the standards of the time as governed by the Judges' Rules, discussed above. The appeal, however, took place in 1988, following the passing and implementation of the Police and Criminal Evidence Act 1985 which, with its Codes of Practice, significantly improved and codified the standards of conduct expected of police officers and did much to improve the protection of the rights of suspects. At the first appeal it would be fair to say that the following facts were established:

- That the defendants had been assaulted or threatened with assault to some extent.

- That they had made their confessions without benefit of legal advice and after a prolonged period of detention.
- That there were serious doubts about the validity of the only real corroborative evidence which were the forensic tests establishing the presence of nitro-glycerine on the hands of some of the defendants.
- That the officers had lied about the timing and sequence of the interrogations.

Judged by the standards of 1988 it would be difficult to see how the confessions could still be admitted with any confidence yet Lord Lane felt able to endorse the original convictions in such unambiguous terms.

From the perspective of a police officer with no inside knowledge of the case it would be fair to deduce the following in 1988:

- If the offence is of such a nature that it outrages public sensibility and there is a continuing threat to society, the police are entitled to 'go the extra mile' in obtaining confessions.
- The officers doing so will be protected and defended by the court.
- Once a suspect is convicted the CPS is entitled to abandon objectivity and support the conviction zealously.
- In the eyes of the courts it may be better that six innocent men remain convicted than that the objectivity and fairness of the English legal system be brought into question.

The Miners' Strike

In 1984–85 Arthur Scargill attempted to close down the whole of the mining industry. He tried to do so without obtaining the support of the whole of his union membership as he was not certain that they would support such an approach. Instead he tried to use the 'flying pickets' tactic which had been so successful in the 1972–73 strike.

It was clear at the outset that this was as much a political as an employment struggle, although Mr Scargill was right about the intentions of the government to remove financial support from the industry. Police were initially used to police the mines in Nottingham where the miners were against the strike. As policing tactics became more and more successful and as the strike grew prolonged, they were then used to protect very small numbers, in one case a single man, returning to work in the Yorkshire pits. I had never known police to give this level of support to such small numbers of workers who were intent on defying strike action. There is no doubt that much of what the flying pickets sought to achieve was illegal and amounted to mob rule. However, it is the duty of the police to enforce the law and protect the rights of the subject even where those rights are inconvenient.

The importance of this case is that the decision-making on strategy and tactics was all done at the highest level of both police and government, the very 'high police command' that Alderson advocates should have the responsibility for formulating the principles of policing and applying the skilled judgement needed to 'avoid harm' and achieve a 'common good'. In policing the legal picketing and demonstrations police tactics included:

- Stopping and turning away pickets and demonstrators a considerable distance from the mines or workplaces targeted. This went so far as to turning back Kent miners at the Dartford Tunnel, some 150 miles from the mines.
- Making a large number of arrests of pickets/demonstrators who were not subsequently proceeded against but who were subject to highly restrictive bail conditions. This effectively prevented them supporting other picket-lines or demonstrations.

The principles that appear to emerge from this experience are:

- The police are entitled, indeed expected, to push the law to and beyond its declared limits if this achieves the operational objective, especially where that operational objective has clear political support from the government.
- The judiciary, in this case in terms of bail conditions and the 'stop and turn away' decision, will endorse and support the police tactics if it appears that some 'greater good' is served.

The Cardiff Three

The brief facts of this case are that a prostitute was found murdered after a frenzied attack in her flat. Five people were initially charged with the murder of whom two were acquitted at the trial. The evidence against the Three was essentially a confession by one incriminating himself and the other two, and that of a number of witnesses who were effectively discredited at the trial. There was no forensic evidence linking the defendants with the murder. Blood, other than the victim's, found at the scene did not match that of any of the three accused. There was also evidence of a suspicious white man with an injured hand in the vicinity of the flat at the time of the murder. The three defendants were black. After arrest one of the defendants, Miller, was interviewed over five days for a total of 13 hours. The interviews were recorded, producing some 19 tapes. Although no solicitor was present for the first two interviews, one was there for the rest.

Miller made some statements which amounted to admissions on tapes 8 and 9, denied the charge over 300 times, but finally made clear admissions on tapes 18 and 19. Four detectives, in various permutations, were involved using a classic 'hard' and 'soft' approach. The Court of Appeal found that the 'hard' approach amounted to bullying and hectoring. The defendant's solicitor was present for all of the relevant interviews and only intervened in the last tape (19). During the course of the trial the judge only listened to part of one tape. That part did not include any of the conduct which the Court of Appeal found to be bullying and hectoring.

In the judgment, Lord Taylor, the Lord Chief Justice, stated about the interviews that 'it is impossible to contain on the printed page the pace, force and manner of the officers' delivery'. Any police officer will find this ironic since following the introduction of tape recorded interviews the police tried in vain to persuade both the CPS and the judiciary of the need to listen to the tapes in order to fully understand the interview. They however took the view that they were used to reading papers quickly and that they would prefer to use a transcript in every case. This created a whole mini-industry in the police service of tape transcribers and summarisers.

The court found that the convictions were unsafe as the confession was clearly obtained by oppression. In this debate the important facts are:

- Throughout the relevant parts of the interview the suspect was represented by a solicitor whose sole purpose was to protect his client's rights.
- The case against 'the Three' was evaluated by the CPS whose decision it was to prosecute, presumably having taken a view on the admissibility of the confessional evidence which was crucial to the potential success of the prosecution.
- Given the defence case raised at trial it was open to the trial judge to listen to any or all of the tapes.
- Defence counsel at trial had the responsibility to ensure that the judge was fully aware of the evidence which would substantiate the defence that the confessional evidence was unsafe.

At the conclusion of the appeal it is noteworthy that the Lord Chief Justice chose to criticise only the police officers and the solicitor present during the interviews. He made no comment on the role of the CPS and went out of his way to praise much of the work of the trial judge.

The issues which arise in this case are:

- Even where the suspect's solicitor, the CPS, the defendant's trial counsel and the trial judge fail to protect the rights of the suspect/defendant, the primary focus for criticism will always be the police.

- Although the CPS have a duty, as officers of the court, to make an objective judgment on the case and thus to have examined all the evidence before instituting or continuing a prosecution, the court would apparently prefer to ignore their role and focus instead on the police when things go wrong (this is unfortunately true also of the media and academic commentators).
- In the judicial process barristers appear to receive a higher level of tolerance for failure than do solicitors.

In most circumstances it is probable that the police, like other principled public servants, will subscribe to Neyroud's eight principles. However, the analysis above shows that, when faced with a genuine dilemma, the working principles which police will use will be pragmatism tempered with the utilitarian concept of some greater good, that greater good being determined by the interpretation that the police officers put on the wishes of government or their perception of the preferred outcome of the criminal justice process. The importance of the cases described above is that they show that this principle applies not just at street level but at every level in policing and that it is an approach which is usually tacitly but sometimes explicitly endorsed by both government and the judiciary. Retired Appeal Court Judge Lord Lawton remarked (*Guardian* 9th July 1991) *'if police are to fill the obligations imposed on them, they have no choice but to bend or break the rules'*.

In many ways government and the criminal justice process rely on the police to interpret the law so as to provide a practical solution to a problem which is difficult to define in purely legal terms. For example, politicians under pressure are often seduced into passing a law which will enable them to claim to have resolved a problem, but then rely on the police to interpret the use of that law so as to make it work in a generally fair way. Two classic examples of this are the unworkable Dangerous Dogs Act, implemented in haste after a spate of attacks by pit bull terriers, and the plethora of legislation which has been passed against trespass, to which the police have had to add conditions concerning the threat to public order before they will act, in order to ensure that it does not impact too severely on genuine travellers. The task is made doubly difficult by the fact that politicians will often give totally contradictory messages. For example, Mr Jack Straw, both as a cabinet minister and backbencher, criticised the police service for failing to act vigorously in dealing with racism in its ranks, yet in a case which attracted massive publicity, he re-instated a police officer who had been sacked (one of the very few ever) for the use of racist language.

It is worthy of note that, according to Waddington (1993), this approach is common to police forces all over the world, despite substantial differences in both political and legal systems. This is not surprising when the nature of the police task is considered objectively. Police officers are asked to work in circumstances of great uncertainty. They are often not able, because of pressures of time and other circumstances, to make a long-considered judgment on the case and are often forced to act with very incomplete information. They are usually dealing with an 'act in progress', be it a riot or an investigation, and cannot conveniently adjourn proceedings to take advice and counsel. In addition it is a police officer's task as an investigator to continually explore new and better ways of establishing the case against the suspect. For example, in dealing with organised crime, it is the essence of the police task to find ways of penetrating and disrupting the criminal organisation. In order to do this it is essential that they are as innovative as possible before even considering whether or not it is proportionate (in the language of the Act) to the rights of the subject e.g. to extend powers to invade privacy by examining bank statements or correspondence, or to covertly eavesdrop, by whatever means, on someone's communications. Having established that these means exist, it is then the police task to put the case for them to legislators. It is they who must then decide whether or not that proportionality does exist.

Where the law is clear the police must obey it. However, there are always instances where it is not clear and in these circumstances it is illogical to expect the investigator to interpret the law in favour of the suspect. The nature of policing is to consider what must be achieved and in the light of that to explore what must be done in terms of what can be done which is legal or is not specifically prohibited. Alternatively, they may need to establish that the circumstances are such that, although it appears that it is specifically prohibited, it may be that the courts will view them as so exceptional that it is permissible. It is then the responsibility of the prosecutor and the court to determine the legality or otherwise of the action.

This was recognised by Lord Denning in *Ghanni v. Jones*, a case of murder where there was no body and the law at the time did not issue search warrants for this offence. In recognising the difficulty this presented the police he said: *'the police have to get the permission of the householder to enter if they can; or, if not, do it by stealth or by force. Somehow they seem to manage. No decent person refuses them permission. If he does he is probably implicated in some way or other. So the police risk an action for trespass. It is not much risk.'* In fact much of the law on the seizure of property as evidence or suspected to be stolen has its origins in police officers doing what they believed to be right in the circumstances but which was not declared as 'lawful' until the common law was changed as a result in either the Court of Appeal or the House of Lords.

Further to this the police often have operational objectives in which the prosecution of an offender is not the primary objective, e.g. the preservation of life, the restoration of order, the development of intelligence; in these circumstances the officer will need to consider whether a breach of the criminal law or a civil tort is 'acceptable' to achieve the operational objective. This was exactly the position regarding covert surveillance before it was legalised. Chief officers had to authorise a breach of the criminal law, criminal damage, and a civil tort, trespass, to enable these operations to go ahead, simply because politicians were unwilling to grasp the nettle of legislating. Under the European Convention on Human Rights (now incorporated in UK law by the Human Rights Act 1988), to which the UK was a signatory, these actions were clearly illegal yet they were endorsed by both the government in the form of a code of practice, and the courts in admitting the evidence obtained.

The fatal weakness of the Alderson/Neyroud approach is that its primary focus always seems to be on the relationship between the suspect and the police, treating the police relationship with others involved as secondary. To use Neyroud's 'Dirty Harry' situation where a kidnap victim is likely to die if not located quickly. The officers have arrested the kidnapper who admits the kidnap, tells the officers of the girl's plight but refuses to tell them her location. Time is running out, in detention terms for the officers and in life terms for the girl. If, in using the eight principles, the girl's right to life is given the primary focus the outcome can be totally different. The situation, though extreme, has all of the features that are a daily part of police decision making. The information is very incomplete; is the girl still alive, does the suspect really know where she is and her state, is she actually under threat at all or in a safe location? There is no time to get better or more complete information before the decision to act must be taken. If the police action is not successful it will be examined with nit-picking hindsight by people who will in the main disregard both the lack of information and the time pressures. No matter how unacceptable it is to the pure-minded philosopher I know that as a police officer my primary concern would be the life of the girl and not the rights of the suspect. What I would do would depend on my interpretation of all of the circumstances. The eight principles would not help me reconcile the key features of the ethics of utility, duty, virtue and care, as I would find myself back to making a personal judgement on what was the 'greater good' based on personal values. These will determine which of the two, the criminal or the victim, has the priority. My actions would depend on what I thought would achieve my desired outcome, saving the girl's life and gaining her freedom. The principles may help me decide how far I can go in balancing those priorities but my actions

74

are more likely to be dependent on what I think will work in all the circumstances.

To proscribe relativism is futile. Any principle which is not absolute is interpreted subjectively according to circumstance. For example Quakers have an absolute principle against taking human life. They will always turn the other cheek regardless of circumstance. Most other Christian beliefs qualify the taking of life with some condition of justifiability, i.e. there is a causal relationship between the principle, the circumstances and the outcome – the outcome is relative to the principle and the circumstances.

It may be that the nature of the policing dilemma is such that pragmatism tempered by crude utilitarianism is the best that can be achieved in practical terms. It can be said that it does provide a buffer between political rhetoric and its consequent, sometimes harsh and discriminatory legislation, affecting minorities (e.g. in trespass and travellers), while at the same time providing a convenient scapegoat for both politicians and lawyers when things go wrong (see Lord Denning supra).

Issues

1. The investigative and enforcement role that the police play makes it essential that they continually explore new ways of improving effectiveness as their current tactics become known and are circumvented. This may make the eight principles described by Neyroud difficult to apply universally and the current principle of pragmatism tempered by utilitarianism may be the only one achievable.
2. The introduction of an 'officer class' or direct entry into senior ranks is unlikely to change this as the pressures for the status quo are not only those of the police. They are an inextricable feature of the policing task and they are endorsed, explicitly and implicitly, by both the government and the criminal justice system.
3. It is convenient for both government and the courts to have police act in this way as it allows them to remain distant from the problem and to have the police act as a buffer (or whipping boy or scapegoat) between them and it.
4. The leadership of the police should have timely access to both ministers and the senior judiciary in order to keep them aware of the explicit and implicit messages they are giving to the service on issues affecting human rights.

The Human Rights Act may not have the effect that is anticipated as:

- The pragmatic principle appears to be a feature of policing universally and is not unique to Britain.

- English judges are conservative as a rule and have tended to be wary of developing too much judge-made law.
- Policing dilemmas usually involve a conflict of human rights and the police are required to make a judgment on whose rights have priority in any given set of circumstances (the relativism that is abhored by the philosopher). This is recognised, at least to some extent, by the test of proportionality in the Convention.

Chapter 5: Organised Crime

Organised crime has been described as the greatest threat to western democracies following the end of the Cold War and the move by the former communist dictatorships towards, in Russia and Eastern Europe, a form of capitalist-based democracy, and, in China, towards a more commercially open and capitalist-based form of totalitarianism. Given this level of threat it is clearly essential that the police for the future should be structured, organised and have tactics and strategies which can give confidence in its ability to deal with this phenomenon.

There does not appear to be a universally agreed definition of 'organised crime'. Taking the words literally, it could describe anything from a small team of burglars working together over time with each responsible for a specific function, e.g. one cases the target, one burgles it and one disposes of the goods, through to a large and complex organisation working on a number of crime fronts transnationally. It is more difficult to describe organised crime in a UK context as we do not have the equivalent of the Italian or Russian Mafia, the Colombian Cartels, the Japanese Yakuza, the Mexican Cartels, the Chinese Triads nor the highly dangerous and violent motorcycle gangs of Scandinavia and North America. In London and one or two other cities we have been exposed to the actions of the Triads and Jamaican posses or yardies and we had been subject to the Nigerian based 419 (the number of the Nigerian statute) letter fraud. In Britain the tradition seems to be much less structured, with individuals or small groups being project-based, i.e. coming together for a specific operation or series of operations and then going their separate ways until the next project is proposed. The growing population of Kurds and Turks and the fairly large Pakistani community are used as a cover for small family clans which use the business and family links between the UK and their homelands as a cover in drugs and human trafficking, but they have not reached the scale of any of the organisations described above.

The main areas for organised crime in the UK are those described in *Understanding Global Issues* (Vol. 99/1) as relating to the world as a whole. They are:

- drugs trafficking
- arms trafficking
- trafficking in people
- smuggling, in the UK it is mainly cigarettes, alcohol and counterfeit goods
- trafficking in wildlife
- fraud, both traditional finance and emerging electronic
- prostitution and pornography
- paedophilia, especially pornographic exchange groups
- loan sharking
- car and plant theft
- counterfeiting, banknotes and goods
- trade in stolen art

The scale of organised crime in these areas ranges from small city-based groups through to globalised transnational criminal organisations. It is difficult to take in the scale of activity. The UN estimates that the net annual returns from organised crime globally is between $1–1.5 billion. The net profits for the Colombian cartels would comfortably sustain that country's national debt. From this it can be seen that these large organisations have the resources with which to take on the forces of law and order in technical, managerial and force-of-arms terms and that they have easily enough resources with which to bribe and corrupt at any level.

From a police perspective a major problem created by the type of crime in which these organisations participate is that most of them are 'victimless'. The difficulty that this creates is that there is no complainant who will bring the crime to police attention. All of the participants have some benefit from the crime and so all are keen to ensure that it is not brought to police attention. This can be true even of major frauds as they are usually directed against large financial institutions and they are more willing to suffer the loss than they are to suffer the adverse publicity. Where there are true victims they are rarely visible to the man in the street in the UK. They themselves, and their families, are very rarely the victim of people trafficking and forced prostitution. Where they are aware of these crimes they are more often than not the purchaser, e.g. of prostitution and pornography of every type, usually produced abroad. Of the crimes listed, only loan sharking impacts directly on the individual in the UK, but this mainly affects the poor and even there provides them access to funds which are otherwise not available. Car and plant theft do have victims but they are usually covered by insurance.

Operational Features of Organised Crime

- The fact that the crime can be described as victimless means that there are no or very few complainants. This means that the nature and extent of the crime can only be uncovered through the use of intensive investigative techniques e.g. infiltration by undercover officers; the development of informants within the organisation; sophisticated surveillance techniques using the whole spectrum of approaches, from officers on the ground through to the use of satellites, all supported by comprehensive and sophisticated intelligence collection and development techniques. The latter two must have a national and transnational capability.

- Even at the lowest level it is unlikely that these organisations will both be based and work in one police area. This is true even of the Metropolitan Police area as the participants are likely to be 'housed' in the suburbs of Kent and Surrey, but work both in the Metropolitan Police area and elsewhere in the country. This cross-border feature makes surveillance, the collection of intelligence and some operational deployment, e.g. with firearms or using covert surveillance techniques, at best cumbersome and often difficult.

- These organisations have high levels of resources: they are rich. This means that they can afford to: both infiltrate and subvert the government and law enforcement bodies; purchase equipment and people for their own protection both in terms of physical defence against the state and other organised criminals and in terms of anti-surveillance techniques.

- The people running these organisations tend to be closer to the clever rather than the stupid end of an intellectual spectrum. This is not the usual target for police work. They are able to distance themselves from the actual criminal activities through layers of management and distribution organisations and the use of self-sufficient cells. They are highly 'surveillance-aware' in terms of both law enforcement agencies and other criminal organisations, and they are able to generate sufficient identities in a sufficient number of countries to ensure that it is difficult, if not impossible, to link the proceeds of crime either directly or indirectly to them.

- They are willing to use high levels of force, including fatal force, if necessary. This can often compensate for a lack of intelligence on their part, makes the development of internal informants difficult and creates a very high risk threshold for undercover officers. Where it is possible to get informants or witnesses it is necessary to support them with a sophisticated witness protection programme, both in order to ensure their safety, and in order to encourage others to come forward. The difficulty and expense in running such a programme is very onerous in terms of most police budgets. It requires a significant investment in staffing: sophisticated liaison with other organisations which have to generate and deal with the false identity; a support programme which keeps the witness separate from family and other former connections; and it leaves the law enforcement body open to a continuous stream of demands from the protected witness which need to be resolved successfully if the programme is not to be undermined.

- They are highly mobile in terms of both their own ability to move nationally and internationally, and their ability to move their profits nationally and internationally. The creation of the European Union and its expansion has massively assisted in this in terms of personal mobility and the removal of international barriers to capital movements which has created a laissez-faire environment where the money launderer is spoilt for choice. This means that it is relatively straightforward for those involved to remove themselves from jurisdictions in which they are wanted or suspected and to sustain themselves whilst abroad through the funds which they have already deposited there. They are thus able to avoid those jurisdictions where controls are tight and they continually seek out the weakest links in terms of avoidance of extradition and surveillance of themselves and their money.
- Those involved in medium or high-level organisations are also engaged in legitimate business (albeit that they have been funded initially from crime). This makes it difficult to separate out legitimate from illegitimate profits and makes the issue of the seizure of assets a particularly difficult one, especially when the assets are in another jurisdiction.

The Position in the UK

As already described there are no mafia equivalents in the UK at this time. There is, however, still a significant problem of organised gangs working in the whole spectrum of activities described, organised on a much more local and smaller scale, but on a geographical basis bigger than most forces and with the connections needed with these larger organisations to manage the local 'outlets'. In addition there is a significant problem with organised gangs involved in 'ram-raiding' (driving a large, usually 4 wheel drive, vehicle through a shop window or arcade doorway and stripping out the store in the three to five minutes inevitable time-lag before police can respond), post office robberies and lorry hi-jacking. All of the difficulties that arise in terms of investigative powers, intelligence, surveillance, financial tracking and witness protection apply equally to this level of crime although limited to the narrower geography of Scotland, Northern Ireland and, because of the historical links, the Republic of Ireland.

In addition, single issue activist groups, the current major one being involved in animal rights, are organised nationally. The internet and mobile phones have provided them with excellent communication and command and control systems which enable them to focus their efforts at very short notice on selected targets. These groups at their extreme are another form of terrorism and share most of the features described above with organised crime (other than money laundering and the use of fatal force, although even here the 'acceptable' threshold is gradually being raised). Currently their use of force is directed at those involved in animal experimentation, but the history of extremism indicates strongly that it is only a matter of time before their own internal dissidents and the police also become 'legitimate' targets.

Although not strictly 'organised crime', cross-border murders, i.e. where the body is found in one force area while the action and suspected perpetrators are in another, present many of the same issues. Although the service is better organised to deal with serial murders and rapes which take place in more than one force area, the process of investigation and information exchange is still a long way from being 'seamless', especially in the early stages of a series or where there are significant gaps between crimes.

The Market

Almost all the crime discussed here involves a market, i.e. the criminals are providing a product or a service which is illegal but for which there is a demand. In any market there are three component parts, demand, supply and price. (Figure 1.) Enforcement is usually directed at both supply and demand. In drugs the majority of enforcement is directed at supply. At a strategic level it has been decided that this is the key element and it is where the majority of resources are aimed. In enforcement terms demand is only controlled by local disruption of activities by divisional level police and even here there is a strong move to decriminalise mere possession for one's own use. This must significantly reduce the impact of these disruption activities in terms of demand. However, the strategy which focuses on supply must accept the market's dynamics. As long as demand remains constant or grows, changes in supply will only affect price. If the enforcement activity is successful and supply is reduced (and that does not appear to have been the case for the last decade where increases in seizures have not led to increases in price) then all that can happen is that either the price increases and

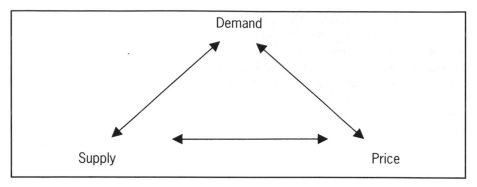

Figure 1: The market

attracts new suppliers or, as existing suppliers are arrested and their organisations disrupted, new suppliers step in to take their place.

It can be seen from this analysis that the key issue is not supply but demand. Despite massive increases in seizures worldwide as well as in the United Kingdom, according to the National Criminal Intelligence Service (NCIS intelligence bulletin No. 9, Autumn 2000), prices of most drugs have come down in cash terms in the period between 1993 and 2000, and all have come down in real terms when inflation is taken into account. In that same time the number and variety of organised groups involved in the drugs trade has grown. In the light of this it can be said that the strategy focused on reducing supply is unlikely to be successful in the longer term. All of the 'vital signs', (i.e. indicators which are not exactly outcomes but which show that there is a general movement towards achieving an outcome), are that the strategy is not working. Since price is only an outcome of the interaction between supply and demand , and the focus on supply does not appear to be workable, it is logical to deduce that the key element in strategic terms is demand.

Demand

Any individual's willingness to engage in illegal activity will depend on the balance to be struck between three elements; the gain or satisfaction to be achieved, the likelihood of being caught and the severity of the consequences of being caught. (Figure 2). If the pleasure or gain has a high value, the individual will be willing to tolerate high probabilities of being caught, coupled with severe punishment. If the gain is small, the likelihood of being caught high and the severity of punishment is also high, it will not be attractive to most people. In terms of drugs there are two separate demand profiles. The first concerns 'soft' drugs which are used in a recreational way

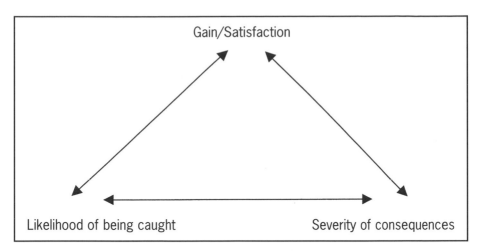

Figure 2: Demand

and which have no physical or psychological addiction. Here pleasure or satisfaction has a low to medium impact, i.e. the individual can live without the drug. The likelihood of being caught is very small and consequences are negligible, especially if it is a first offence. In order to increase the probability of being caught it would be necessary to significantly increase police numbers and police activity in this area; to introduce fairly draconian powers of search and to impose duties and responsibilities on the owners of licensed premises and places of public entertainment which may be unacceptable or unenforceable. In these circumstances, to increase the severity of punishment would only create martyrs and it is unlikely that such an approach could sustain public support. The key element is thus the element of pleasure or satisfaction. This could be addressed through the education system, through continuous public education in its broadest sense, and through a deliberate propaganda-style approach intended to change attitude. Project Charlie, a drug prevention programme for primary school children in Hackney, ran between 1991 and 1993, and showed that this could be achieved through the education system. The key question is why it was not then extended throughout London at least? The success of the drink/drive campaigns and the safe sex campaign to reduce the impact of AIDS show what can be achieved if the resources and the political will are there. The deteriorating situation as far as safe sex is concerned, especially with young people, shows the absolute necessity to be willing to sustain the message over time, and to continually revisit it and to re-address it in the light of changing circumstances.

The current approach is totally unsatisfactory. There is no nationally agreed or approved approach to drugs education. In fact a number of forces and education authorities are following programmes which have been proved empirically to be ineffective (O'Connor et al., 1999). In light of the nature of the threat, the level of research and support in this area is woefully inadequate. The current government strategy does not identify the resources of a scale and focus which are likely to change the situation in either the short or the longer term. There is no provision at all for public education in its broadest sense nor is there evidence of a willingness to develop and support a focused campaign to change attitudes. Indeed, if the approach to tobacco is to be taken as any guide it seems that no government is able to sustain a focused and effective effort in the face of resilient commercial opposition. The approach to tobacco is a good indicator of the key importance of political will. In the 1980s and 1990s this was the focus of significant attention and there was a reduction its use, particularly by men both old and young. That focus was not successful with women and we have now reached the stage where there are more young women smoking than young men. The issue of political will is crystallised by the public face of cigarette smoking. At one time there appeared to be a self-imposed ban, in both television and advertising, to cigarette smoking. That ban seems to have been removed and it is difficult to believe it is coincidental that the main smokers are glamorous young women or people engaged in dramatic and attractive roles. In the light of the government's inability to sustain a campaign here, where the effect on health is obvious and agreed, where the sale is taxed and produces significant revenues which could be used to sustain a reduction strategy, and where the government has the power to control explicit and implicit advertising, it is difficult to believe that the political will is there to make any significant impact on the use of soft drugs.

The approach to drugs which have addictive properties, either physical or psychological, is necessarily different. Here the pleasure or satisfaction element has a high impact. It is unlikely that a significant increase in the likelihood of being caught is enough in itself to deter. Even if this were so it would have the same consequences in civil liberties terms as that described for 'soft' drugs. It is also doubtful that merely increasing the severity of consequences would have a sufficiently deterrent effect and, in my view, there are ethical difficulties in punishing an individual for what can be fairly described as an illness. It is incongruous that society treats the alcoholic with sympathy and support, while at the same time treating drug addiction as a criminal offence for which the addict must be punished.

The clear strategic need is to reduce or eliminate demand. To do this it is necessary to reduce or eliminate the effects of addiction—and this can be done. There is absolutely no doubt that treatment works. The empirical proof is overwhelming and has been demonstrated time and again in studies in the UK, the US and Australia. These show that re-offending can be significantly reduced both in terms of drug usage and acquisitive crime, that the period between offences can be lengthened significantly and that there are significant benefits for both the criminal justice system and health service in cost reductions due to the reduction of offending and in an improved lifestyle. (A useful summary of the research is found in *Drug-Driven Crime*, National Association for the Care and Resettlement of Offenders, 1999.) Despite this, the availability of treatment is still very variable in terms of access, quality of treatment, effectiveness of approach, willingness to offer treatment to those who failed first time (a key feature given that drug misuse is a chronic relapsing condition) and of the availability and effectiveness of 'gateways' in custody centres and courts. In prisons, where government controls all of the variables, the availability and effectiveness of treatment is patchy (whereas the availability of drugs appears to be pervasive) and there are no nationally agreed transition arrangements from prison back to the community. Prisons have provided a salutary lesson on the complexity of the drugs issue and on the dangers of adopting a simplistic approach by the introduction of the compulsory drug-testing programme. The Howard League for Penal Reform found that a significant number of prisoners were opting to use heroin rather than cannabis in prisons purely because testing could discover cannabis for a period of 10 to 14 days after use, whereas with heroin the test would be negative after 24 hours. In this way testing may be reducing the volume of drug use but is actually increasing the harm to the individual and, because heroin is less likely to be detected, the approach will appear to be 'successful' as a reduced number of prisoners will be identified as using. The League went so far as to propose that the use of cannabis in prisons should be ignored if the testing regime was to be continued, creating the ironic situation where an activity would be criminal outside prison but not inside.

The current government has developed a widely-based strategy which they stated was intended to build on that developed by the previous one. It seeks to improve significantly those elements of education and treatment and has allocated significant funding to the programmes. A major difficulty with it is that the targets which it has set are manifestly unachievable e.g. 'to reduce the proportion of people under 25 using heroin and cocaine by 25 per cent by 2005 and by 50 per cent by 2008'. To a practitioner it appears highly improbable that the most sophisticated programme could so significantly reverse a trend in such a short period of time. In addition, at the time the target was set, neither the base data were known with any certainty, nor had the programmes which would seek to achieve this massive change been tested in any meaningful way. As stated earlier, there is a real need to set targets if progress is to be made in any field. However, if they are to be effective they must be achievable; if they are to be achievable there must be some certainty about both the baseline data, the reliability of the statistics and the effectiveness of the methodology. The current approach is correct in principle but very poor in practice. There is a consequent danger that much of the good work which is being and will be done, will be denigrated and undermined by the impossibility of the targets now set.

Ideal Force Capabilities

Given this description of organised crime in general and drugs in particular, it is possible to formulate a capability profile for an enforcement agency which can best deal with it and then compare that against the actual capability in the UK.

Enforcement

- The ability to move freely nationally and transnationally with extensive investigative powers. This must be accompanied by an ability to liaise and work with foreign enforcement agencies at every level.
- A comprehensive and sophisticated surveillance capability in terms of both people and technical equipment.
- A comprehensive national and transnational intelligence system which contains information and intelligence on operators and organisations from street level to transnational level.
- A comprehensive and transnational capability to track financial transactions and to make seizures with the minimum notice to the relevant judicial authorities so as to minimise notice given to the suspect.
- A change to the burden of proof in offences of trafficking so that once a level of possession or level of participation in the working of an organisation is established, being engaged in trafficking becomes a rebuttable presumption with the burden of proof for that rebuttal passing to the defendant.
- A change to the working of the Inland Revenue so that it becomes part of the criminal investigation process and uses its powers, where it is established the suspect was living beyond their visible means, to assume a level of income and from that establish the crime of tax evasion. Ideally this should be done transnationally but there would be significant if not insuperable problems in establishing this.

Demand reduction

- An ability to focus the service's own resources together with those of other agencies on those factors which can be proved to reduce demand so as to provide a more uniform national approach.
- A national strategy which is based on approaches for which there is empirical proof of efficacy; in which the roles of the major agencies are clearly defined and for which there is real accountability in terms of outcomes. It is unlikely that this can be achieved without the use of a mechanism such as a Royal Commission.

The Current Position in the UK

Police

There are 43 police forces in England and Wales, eight in Scotland and the Royal Ulster Constabulary (RUC). For these forces there are three policy sources, the Association of Chief Police Officers (ACPO), the Association of Police Authorities (APA) and government. The RUC is part of ACPO but has a separate government structure. The Scottish forces have a separate ACPO and take their government direction from the Scottish Office but overall there is reasonable coherence in the policies followed in each country. When examined in light of the capabilities described above however, the weakness of the current structure becomes all too apparent.

Enforcement

Mobility
Before the UK police can look at transnational ability we need to deal with the serious issue of internal mobility. Scotland and Northern Ireland have different legal systems and devolved governments. This means that police officers do not have full police powers outside of their national jurisdiction and always require the co-operation and support of the local police in order to carry out any action. Customs and Excise do not suffer this restriction. The situation in the UK crystallises the difficulty that will be met when trying to move with the UK and other nations to a more transnational basis of policing. England and Scotland have been united under one crown since 1704, and one parliament since 1807. Only within each of their jurisdictions do police officers have full powers and even here will normally only act having informed the local forces of their intentions. Local chief constables still have an effective power of veto over other forces, although not the National Crime Squad (NCS), in terms of firearms operations or operations in those communities where sensitivities are high.

Surveillance
This is a very expensive police activity. In order to track the 'surveillance aware' suspect for 16 hours a team of between 12 and 16 is needed, depending on the likely movements of the suspect. Technical equipment and advanced intelligence of likely movements can reduce this cost, but generally only at the margin. The average size of forces in England and Wales is 1,600 to 2,000 officers. In Scotland, outside of Strathclyde, it is significantly smaller. The RUC, because of its history, has a formidable surveillance capability. Most forces have a very limited surveillance capability, usually limited to two or three teams. These generally have to cover the whole gamut of surveillance activity from serious criminals suspected of property crime such as robbery and burglary, through drugs, and in some forces also encompassing Special Branch activity. They have not been encouraged to develop their own technical surveillance capability but have been pushed to rely instead on using 'pooled' equipment held by one force or that supplied by the NCS. Most officers are given basic surveillance training but the standard in forces is variable and, given its cost, the commitment to it as an activity overall is also variable, often dependent on annual budgetary requirements.

Intelligence
Every force has a central intelligence bureau, but the bulk of the intelligence activity is carried out by basic command units and is focused at a very local level. Very few forces have the capability of giving other forces immediate access to their intelligence records and a significant number of forces do not even have the capability of providing 24-hour access in-force. This means that operational officers are unnecessarily deprived of access to what can be vital information and that there is an inevitable delay in the updating of information. Forces do not have open access to the National Criminal Intelligence Service (NCIS) systems but can only gain this through its operatives. This is not a criticism as this is a necessary security and filtration gateway. Again the quality of information held and the quality of analytical capability in forces are highly varied. There are no national standards of competency or training in this key area and a significant part of the work is done by civilians who may not be able to recognise any deficiency, if it exists, in their police line manager's analytical capability in terms of interpreting the base information.

Financial tracking and seizure
This reflects the picture for intelligence and surveillance with each force trying to sustain small teams of variable ability through the ups and downs

of budget changes and difficulty in recruiting to a very narrowly-based task: an impossible one for those forces foolish enough to try to follow the Home Office requirements on tenure of service. This requires forces to move officers through specialist roles within a set period (tenure), usually three to five years, returning them as a matter of routine to general police duties. Its aim is to ensure that officers are always able to be returned to general duties and, according to the Home Office and the HMIC, it brings the specialist skills back into general police duties. In describing it I am reminded of Kenneth Galbraith's description of President Regan's 'trickle-down' economics as trying to get oats to sparrows by overfeeding a horse. There is no doubt that it will have some of the benefits described but of one hundred ways of doing it the proposal comes one hundred and first. No other organisation is expected to spend vast amounts of time and money training its people in specialist skills only to move them away from the work just at the point where the organisation is gaining the maximum return on that training and experience.

Liaison and information exchange
The UK is fairly unique in not having a national police force. Each force is independent of the other and only the Metropolitan Police, and Kent, due to the Channel Tunnel, have a real international capability. Indeed the absence of a national force leads foreigners to treat the Met as if it were one. This makes liaison difficult both ways and means that investigators are forced to work through the NCS and NCIS, unless they have fortuitously managed to set up a bilateral arrangement with the foreign force. When this factor is combined with the sensitivities of all governments and judiciaries to foreign forces carrying out any tasks within their jurisdiction, it puts the UK service at a particular disadvantage when dealing with matters which have an international aspect.

NCS and NCIS
Until 1995 the UK had no national capability in terms of intelligence, surveillance or investigation. The highest level of capability was delivered by the Regional Crime Squads (RCS) which had grown out of the Task Forces developed by groups of forces in the 1970s to deal with cross-border crime. This informal arrangement was formalised by the development of the RCS. There was no direct entry into the squads and they were made up of officers on secondment from forces. The work that the RCS encompassed became national rather than regional crime and by the time of the formation of the NCS it could be fairly said that the bulk of their work was either at a national or international level. This has left the service with a serious and growing gap at regional or cross force level as most forces do not have the

capability to deal with this level of crime, and the NCS has too many more serious targets to be able to take this work on. The formation of the NCS is an interesting case study in how difficult it can be to develop consensus with 43 chief officers. A minority of chief officers were in total opposition to the setting up of the NCS, believing that it would undermine the position of the regular forces. The concept of an NCS was discussed for some five to ten years before it was possible to overcome this opposition and set it up, despite the fact that it was clear that it had become a national organisation in fact if not in terms of its constitutional definition: all it lacked was the appropriate management and tasking structure. However the manner in which it was set up meant that the NCIS was created separately, although logic demands that the intelligence and operational capability should come under a unitary command.

Both of these bodies are staffed by recruiting police officers on secondment from forces, although it would appear that the case has now been made by the NCS for direct recruitment, partly due to the difficulty in recruiting from regular forces and partly because forces are more and more unwilling to second officers for the five to ten years that the NCS believe are necessary in terms of overall efficiency. This may improve the internal working of the NCS but it will mean that the bridge created by the seconded staff will be considerably weakened, with a consequential drift growing between the NCS, NCIS and the forces. There is already tension growing between the NCS and NCIS and the forces on the subject of funding, where the former are using their position of direct access to ministers to make the case for considerable growth at the expense of the forces.

The political oversight of the organisations has also presented a problem. The RCS were overseen by regional boards on which each of the member police authorities were represented. Each board was chaired by a police authority member and there was at least the semblance of political oversight with the interests of the forces being a major consideration. This is not possible with a national body and it is clear that the Association of Police Authorities (APA) do not feel that they are able to influence key decisions, such as funding, in the way that was possible in the days of the RCS. Logic and history point to a growing central direction and control of these bodies.

The NCIS was formed in 1995 in response to the need for the police to be able to gather and analyse intelligence at a national and international level and in order to create a policing body which had the same parameters as Customs and Excise. There had been a long history of suspicion and lack of co-operation between Customs and Excise and some police forces. The purpose of the NCIS was to provide an interface between the services where both could be confident in how information was stored and disseminated. It has been a successful concept and, unlike the NCS, is the closest thing that the service has to a truly 'national' organisation.

In intelligence terms there remains the major difficulty that the enforcement bodies, of whatever ilk, tend to keep back little bits of information on the grounds that they are still 'working them up' and that they are not quite ready to be shared, especially if the holder believes that there might be a 'body' (an arrest) in it. The profusion of intelligence units within forces at Basic Command Unit (BCU) level, each serving teams with this attribute and having it themselves; the fact of 43 force-level intelligence units; the fact that some are not computer supported and thus access must be limited to physical searches; the fact that Customs and Excise is a totally separate organisation with a separate agenda answering to a separate minister, makes it highly unlikely that the service is maximising the return that it is possible to get from the intelligence function.

The security services
At the end of the Cold War the security services became involved in providing intelligence on international organised crime with the intention of providing that information for internal use for the first time. The nature of terrorism, both cause-based and state-sponsored, meant that they would have had to do so for their own counter intelligence role in any case as there is a strong link between terrorism and organised crime in arms, drugs and people-trafficking. At the time it looked as if the service would have spare capacity. However, the collapse of the Balkans and the Russian empire in Eastern Europe and Asia with its consequent nuclear threat and the continuing uncertainty on the outcome of the peace process in Ulster, make it difficult to believe that their impact is anything other than marginal at this time.

Issues

1. It will not be possible to check or reverse the illegal drugs trade by enforcement alone in the foreseeable future (10–20 years). The mechanics of the market and the scale of profit will defeat this approach. Demand is the key strategic issue. The logical approach is one that tries to limit supply and expansion of the market while at the same time working on the factors that affect demand.
2. Whilst there has been a significant increase in the resources devoted to enforcement, that has not been matched by those devoted to reducing demand.

3. There is an urgent need to find out what works in influencing people generally, and young people in particular, to choose not to become users and then to adequately fund, support and sustain programmes aimed at achieving this.
4. There is an urgent need to provide uniform and adequately funded treatment for addicts based on what is known to work.
5. The current police structure is not suitable to deal with organised crime, either nationally or internationally based. It is unlikely that changes in systems and processes alone can overcome this structural weakness.
6. The current structure cannot deal effectively with cross-border/regional crime and it is unlikely that forces will feel able to fund a new version of the regional crime squad, nor will they be willing for the NCS to be funded to do so if this is at the expense of forces. The 'upward drag' of serious national and international crime will inevitably mean that such provision will be used by the NCS to fund work in this area.

Chapter 6: Performance: Stochastic Frontier Analysis (SFA) and All That

Policing is no different from any other organisation in that it is important that it continuously improves its performance, i.e. produces the same for less, produces more with less, ensures that any increase in resources is at least matched by an improvement in service. The difficulties in improving performance are very much those of any service-driven organisation. Improving performance in production may be as difficult as in service organisations, but it is at least more straightforward in that there are usually fewer variables which affect output. As well as all of the difficulties which any service organisation has in improving performance, the police service has a number which are unique and which arise out of the nature of the police task itself which is focused on the enforcement of law and its consequent potential infringement on the rights of the individual. In dealing with performance there appear to be nine major difficulties faced by the British police service. They are:

- the nature of policing itself
- the culture
- ethics
- the difficulty in establishing a causal link between inputs and outputs and then outcomes
- the lack of performance management skills
- the lack of an agreed database
- the lack of input and financial data for activity based costing
- the critical dependency for strategic shifts on effective partnerships with other public agencies
- the confusion of priorities and messages given by external stake-holders

The Police Task

In terms of performance management policing is unique in two respects. Firstly, some of the work involves law enforcement: it is a service that is delivered against the wishes of the service recipient. In carrying out this task the police officer is asked to make a judgement about how invasive the state can be in affecting the rights of the individual, those actions ranging from simple traffic direction all the way through to being locked up incommunicado. Any organisation can only be bettered through the improvement in the performance of the individuals who make it up, the more so where the work is very labour intensive. Thus the police leader is left with the dilemma of knowing that it is essential to measure individual performance, whilst at the same time knowing that the mere fact of measuring activity may encourage, stimulate or implicitly coerce an officer to act in a particular way. The decision to do so is based on management requirements (getting a tick in a box), rather than the circumstances. Experience in policing, and of any other organisation where performance management techniques are used, powerfully shows that when robust performance management comes in the door, ethics tend to go out through the window. These factors make any suggestion of performance-related pay, at any level in the service, an extremely dangerous and foolish one.

Those whose performance is being measured will move through a range of tactics to avoid, subvert or superficially satisfy the measurement regime. The first usual reaction is merely to question the basic data, especially if it is unfavourable. The next is to sustain the same working practices but find ways of describing and reporting on them so as to satisfy the performance regime. Focusing on those elements of the new regime which are most easily satisfied and where compliance is likely to leave the rest of the individual's working practices alone usually follows this. If all that is done is to bring in a measurement regime, then it is likely that the workforce will try to concentrate its efforts on these elements alone at the expense of concentrating on what is important but is either difficult to achieve and/or difficult to measure. For example, in Bedfordshire when we began to measure the effectiveness in dealing with emergency calls and questioned the basic workload of officers as reflected in the number of recorded calls from the public, the first response of officers was that the level of work was significantly higher than that actually recorded and that the calls recorded on the Operational Information System were not a true reflection of officers' workload. When we sought to improve the effectiveness of the intelligence system, the immediate response was to inundate the Local Intelligence Officers with written intelligence reports, for which the officer was given credit regardless of the actual content of the report. As soon as quality controls were introduced the numbers reduced considerably. This effect can have unforeseen beneficial outcomes. I had for years been trying to get officers to take domestic violence seriously without much success. As soon as detections became a measure of performance the attitude to domestic violence changed. They began to be recorded, at last, as crimes, not because officers had a sudden change of attitude towards domestic violence, but because, as the assailant was known, an easy detection could be claimed. This made it much easier to measure the actual level of domestic violence in the community and then to set arrest parameters that significantly improved the service given to victims.

Domestic violence itself crystallises some of the other problems in measuring effectiveness. If the measure of effectiveness is the satisfaction of the victim, it is unlikely that this will be met merely by arrest. The availability of refuges, the willingness of local authority housing departments or housing associations to treat the woman as the tenant and thus evict the man, the willingness of the CPS to sustain the prosecution, the willingness of the magistrates to impose effective bail conditions and deterrent sentences, will all have a much higher impact on the victim's overall level of satisfaction than the initial police action, albeit that this is the key to opening the access door to all of these other factors. A meaningful measurable outcome on overall effectiveness may be the frequency with which police are called back to this particular family. Given the factors described above, it can be seen that this is more likely to be achieved by the action of other agencies rather than police alone. It is therefore unrealistic to measure police effectiveness by this measure.

If the simple measurement criteria of arrest is taken, it can be seen that, unless it is part of a complex and interrelated matrix of factors, not only will it be impossible to measure performance by focusing on one factor of a complex matrix, but doing so is likely to skew performance at the expense of those factors not measured. These factors will include:

- Whether or not the crime is one that is tactically or strategically important to the division.
- The adequacy of the evidence at the time of arrest and obtained subsequently.
- The fair treatment of the suspect.
- The preparation of a prosecution file which was acceptable to the CPS.
- The efforts put into the arrest by the officer; i.e. was it made as a result of considerable effort on their part in the investigation, or merely someone given into custody by a witness such as a store detective.

The only way in which these factors can be dealt with is to ensure that the police at every level have the same values. In this way the officer, in making the arrest, will be aware of the need to ensure that:

- Time, the only truly scarce resource, is used to best effect and it is not done to gain a tick in some bean-counter's box.
- It was not carried out until they had enough evidence to support the arrest and had reasonable confidence that prosecution could be sustained.
- The legal rights of the suspect should be protected throughout the process.
- His right to dignity as a human being would be respected.
- The case will be put fairly to CPS with full disclosure of all the evidence, including that which was favourable to the suspect or unfavourable to the prosecution.
- The officer would focus their efforts on the development of effective intelligence and sound investigations rather than merely seeking targets of opportunity for which they achieved maximum personal benefit for the least effort.

To find out whether or not this is likely to be the case it is necessary to look at the culture of the service.

Culture

It is clear from what has gone before that the success or otherwise of any attempt to improve police performance will be critically dependent on a sharing of values at every level. The history of policing is littered with comments by politicians, community leaders, academics and journalists that whilst the intentions and policies of senior officers came close to reflecting that which was needed in the circumstances, these policies were not reflected in the actual practices of police officers on the ground. This is an inevitable outcome where the values that underpin those policies are held by the leadership alone and are not shared by the whole organisation. An alternative interpretation which I believe is too often correct is that the actual behaviour of the leadership shows that they share the same values as the rest of the organisation and have developed policies due to political necessity rather than personal belief: an implicit signal that the organisation can ignore them if operational necessity dictates. These issues are discussed in greater detail in Chapter 4 on equality.

Reiner (Reiner, 1996) has described the culture of the police service at length and while some of the factors described have become less stark, I

Table 1: Reiner's core characteristics of police culture as summarised by Neyroud and Beckley (2001)

Reiner's 'core characteristics' of police culture.	Core characteristics of a balanced performance culture.
A sense of mission, which is primarily seen as 'action' led.	A sense of mission, which is based on reflection and shared values.
Cynicism or pessimism about the world and those they deal with.	A realistic belief that it is possible to make a difference.
Suspicion, which is partly a product of the need to categorise and discriminate those they confront, but is also encouraged by the training and socialisation process.	Openness to criticisms and new ideas.
Isolation and solidarity, a combination of social isolation and solidarity and loyalty to colleagues in the face of danger from external threat.	Value-driven, staying alert to the tensions created by the need to improve performance and the need to balance that with strong adherence to values in order to avoid the introduction of corrupt practices.
Conservative, seen partly as a product of the role, upholding the status quo, and partly related to the stability of the organisation and its enforced neutrality.	Innovative, continually looking for ways to improve and ways to learn from the success or failure of others.
Machismo, which was evidenced by the hard drinking and aggressive sexuality of many male officers.	Recognition of worth and potential to contribute regardless of gender, sexual orientation etc.
Racially prejudiced, some of which Reiner links to the dominant attitude of the majority towards minorities, some to the transactional relationships between police officers and minorities they police against.	Balanced and fair, with a clear understanding of how policing can affect the human rights of others.
Pragmatic.	Future-oriented, using past performance in a non-blaming environment in order to inform future actions.

believe that they still fairly describe the 'core characteristics of cop culture'. These characteristics will not only fail to support a performance-driven culture, they will also guarantee that any drive to enhance performance will have a significant and unacceptable impact on the suspect's civil rights and on the service's relationship with the public, especially minorities. The difference between the current police culture and that needed to sustain a fair and balanced approach to improving performance is described in the table above.

The gap between these two paradigms is enormous, especially in the issues of openness, reflection, values and future-orientation, key components if performance improvement is to be balanced with rights. To move from the current paradigm to the ideal would require strong management skills both in performance and change management.

Management Skills

The management skills of the service reflect the culture. In my experience police officers are excellent crisis managers and can quickly restore order from chaos, exercising all the skills required to do that in terms of courage, decision-making, communication, short-term planning, motivation and operational leadership. There are three key areas where change is required in terms of skills and one in terms of values, where the service has an urgent need to introduce change and improvements. The three skills areas are numeracy, strategic (as opposed to tactical) planning and problem-solving.

Numeracy

Given the large number of variables which effect police performance, it is clearly essential that managers have sound, if not excellent, numeracy skills if they are to understand what the numbers are telling them. From my experience in selecting officers, both in-force and at a national level, I have found that, whereas they have sound critical thinking and verbal skills, there is a pervasive weakness in the area of numeracy. This is known by all those involved in selection at least at the national level. Despite this there is almost no additional or specialist training given in police management courses in this key area. In Bedfordshire I had to introduce my own additional training (provided by the Police Foundation) in order to fill this gap. This factor limits effectiveness as a financial manager and, taken together with the lack of sophisticated finance and incident information systems, has made it extremely difficult to develop activity-based costing (ABC). The development of this is essential for making predictive decisions at a force level and dealing with the constant pressure from the Treasury for a demonstrable link between inputs and outputs.

Strategic planning

Most officers at superintendent level are sound tactical planners but only a relatively small number are good strategic planners, i.e. able to see what is needed in the medium to long-term, and to make the necessary provision in terms of personnel, skills and budget to satisfy that strategic need. Below the rank of superintendent at inspector level, the key rank in terms of day-to-day operations, the planning is usually limited to day-to-day or at best a week-on-week basis, with little thought given to the medium term needs of the unit. This is so even when the advantages of such planning are drawn to their attention. The failure to plan in this way means that these officers are continually ambushed by shortages in skills and resources.

Problem-solving and reflection

I have written elsewhere (O'Byrne, 1997) on the need for managers at every level, but especially inspector level, to reflect on what has worked or not worked and what can be learned from that. To introduce problem solving and reflection it is necessary to gain control of time and to create a virtuous circle involving time, attitude and skills. Officers who are busy are reluctant to give up time to learn new, non-traditional skills (e.g. reflection, statistical analysis) even if those new skills are essential for dealing with the workload more effectively. Since there is no visible model of success, there is little confidence that the skills will make the difference claimed and anyway there will be no time to put them into practice. The lack of planning skills needed means that they have difficulty in creating the time to learn the new skills and to benefit from putting them into practice. In addition, since they have not thought out what they could do differently in order to do it better, they see little benefit in the exercise.

A final nail in the coffin is the fact that the development of 'fundamental' solutions usually requires a willingness to live with a delay while new skills are developed. This runs against the culture's need for immediate action, i.e. 'quick' rather than sustainable fixes. This usually leads the service to deal with deep-seated problems on a symptomatic rather than endemic issues basis. In his book *The Fifth Discipline*, Senge (1992, p112) describes in systems terms the problems that this creates. (Figure 3). An example of this in practice is the introduction of crime desks into forces. The public complaints usually concerned difficulty in reporting, and learning the results of, poor (often non-existent) investigation. Most officers recognised that the real deep-seated problem in dealing with crime was that of poor investigation and problem solving. The introduction of crime desks only improved reporting and recording, it had no effect on investigation or problem solving. It had however the negative side effect of taking the immediate supervisors

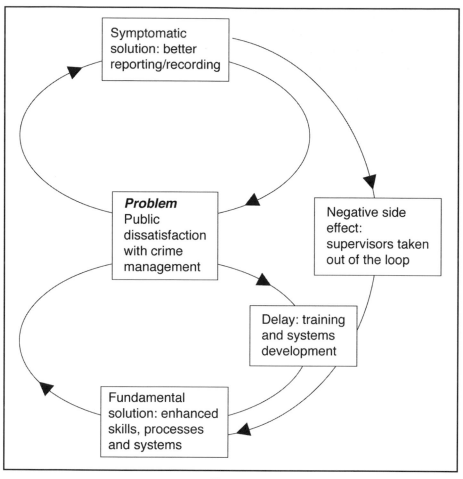

Figure 3

out of the line, with officers submitting crime reports directly to the crime desks. This created the 'double-whammy' of both removing the line manager's ability to control quality, and of absolving them of responsibility for it.

Database Difficulties

The difficulty which the service has with compiling and using a comprehensive and accurate database, has a number of roots. There is the antipathy to the use of numbers already described. This is compounded by the historical use of statistics in the service. It is only in the last five to ten years that the service has collected information for analytical use by the force itself, rather than merely as a collecting agency for other organisations. Traffic data was gathered in the main for use and analysis by highways authorities; crime data was always historically collected for the Home Office for national publication, very little use was made of the information in force. The explosion of performance indicators which has taken place in the last five to ten years, has meant that forces have gradually built up more comprehensive databases, but again the driver has been external rather than internal and much of the debate has been, not on the operational usefulness of the data gathered, but rather on ensuring that the same definition and description is used for comparison across forces. This has not been helped by the tendency of the Home Office to change the goalposts during the process, e.g. the changes in the recorded crime 'counting rules', which have made comparison (a key element of *Best Value*) extremely difficult. Very few forces have comprehensive databases on the key operational issues and hardly any have effective databases on issues that are not part of the national or Best Value performance indicators, for example on the extensive quality of life issues that lie at the heart of police work.

The position is best summarised by looking at the history of 'recorded' crime. These are national statistics gathered by the police for use by the government to decide on the crime 'health' of the country as a whole. Those which can be 'recorded' under the system are defined by the Home Office, which also issues detailed (but not always clear) instructions on how these crimes shall be counted, the Home Office Counting Rules. Forces rarely gathered systematic data on crimes not defined as 'recordable' even if they were important to operational decision making, e.g. minor public order offences. The way that criminal damage has developed over time exemplifies the relative uselessness of this approach. In 1972 an edict came from the Home Office that criminal damage under £20 should not count as a crime: from memory there was no rationale behind either the singling out of this particular offence or the monetary limit set. The proportion of crime 'no-crimed' under this heading remained the same for a considerable period despite the effects of inflation. In addition forces found it attractive to use this 'no-crime' category to disguise other more serious crime. What were clearly attempted burglaries and attempted thefts from or of vehicles were more often than not classified as criminal damage and thus effectively removed from recorded crime. This had the effect of reinforcing those cultural issues of pragmatism, cynicism, isolation and action focus already described as a dysfunctional part of the culture. A second, and equally important effect, was that it removed significant data from the crime database as far as crime patterns were concerned, again undermining the potential effectiveness of an analytical approach. Although the example given is an 'old chestnut' in police terms the practice still goes on in forces, to the extent that HMIC felt the need to comment on it (HMIC, 1998).

No force that I am aware of has a comprehensive relational database of key activities which allows managers to analyse the effectiveness of police activities and which will enable them to anticipate changes and make 'predictive' decisions. By this I mean being able to move resources from one area of activity to another with the confidence that the resources moved will have a quantifiable beneficial effect in the area to which they have been moved, and that the manager has some certainty on the effect, beneficial or otherwise, on the area from which they are removed. For example, to move uniformed officers from patrol or response to work on a vehicle crime squad with the certain knowledge that it will increase the detections or decrease the offences committed, whilst at the same time knowing the effect that it will have on the ability to manage the response function. In addition, it should be possible to relate all of this to cost so that the relative cost of sustaining any given activity can be described. If this can be done there are two benefits: firstly, the police leader is able to make the 'predictive' decision described above; secondly, it will finally be possible to engage the police authority in making choices for which they can be held accountable. In Bedfordshire we had made considerable progress in the area of activity based costing, but it was a concept which did not have general support or understanding in the service as a whole.

Partnership

The police face two problems in dealing with partner agencies. The first and most important is the fact that in almost any activity in which the police are involved, those factors which are strategic, i.e. need to be affected if the situation is to be changed over time and permanently, are provided by other agencies and are often only incidental or peripheral to that other agency's work. Secondly, most of these other agencies are local government bodies and have a more drawn out and uncertain system of decision-making. The former was recognised by the Morgan Report which was not implemented by the government of the day but is now reflected in the provisions of the Crime and Disorder Act 1998; the latter is not recognised anywhere.

If we take drugs as an example, we have already established that the key strategic issue is demand. There is now a significant body of evidence which shows that a significant amount of acquisitive crime takes place in order to satisfy the needs of those addicted to hard drugs such as heroin (summarised in NACRO, 1999). The NHS is responsible for providing treatment centres. The provision nation wide is very patchy, both in terms of actual centres and in the quality of treatment provided. It is thus possible for a force to do all it can in terms of disrupting local trafficking and in providing a drugs reference process for those arrested and yet fail in this area if the NHS provision means that those referred need to wait for three to six months (or perhaps forever), before being offered treatment. It is even worse when the NHS has provided an effective treatment centre which it then limits or abandons because of budget pressures, as its existence will probably have attracted people from outside the area who then become a local policing problem and for whose criminal activity the police will be blamed. In most strategic issues such as estate planning, street lighting, car design, car park design and staffing, credit card design, etc., the police do not control any of the strategic factors but are expected, through enforcement alone, to make a difference. The committees set up under the Act are a first step towards correcting this problem but thus far the experience is not particularly promising. The NHS seems to have avoided its responsibilities under the Act, both in terms of participating with the local committees and of providing support for the youth offending provisions of the Act. Overall, the participation of local government is very variable, with the enthusiasm for participation appearing to have an inverse relationship to the degree of funding required.

It is in decision-making that the difference between the police and other local government bodies becomes starker. Chief executives do not have anything like the same executive authority as chief constables. Since they do not have the powers they cannot delegate them, whereas it is common practice in the police service for the local divisional or BCU commander to have the ability to commit at least his own unit and usually the force in any bodies where they represent the force. This has become increasingly the case as forces have devolved more and more of their budgets to the BCU. This means that the police can act as soon as a decision is taken. In local government however the situation is very different. It is often the case that the representative is given very limited powers to commit the organisation, sometimes even no powers. In addition it is usually necessary, if resources are required, for them to have to take what is effectively a recommendation back to their councillors in order that politicians can debate it and decide. This is usually done on an incomplete brief since they were not present at the forum where the decision is needed and can mean that the representative then comes back with the decision so qualified that the original body needs to go through the whole decision-making process again and again. Thus a decision which the police can make in days or weeks can often take months and even longer because of the decision-making processes of partners.

Stakeholders

The service entered the 1990s crying out for direction from politicians on what was expected of it and what the public and government saw as being its priorities. It was not passive in this and the staff associations had banded together to commission the Operational Policing Review, an extensive survey, which gave a sound indication of public priorities and reassured the service that in the main it was already focused on what the public saw as being important. There were no objectives or performance indicators, indeed the average police officer would have described a PI as a personal injury road traffic accident rather than a performance indicator. The home secretary then produced his first set of objectives. These were rather vague and were very crime focused. The then home secretary made it clear that he saw the police as being crime fighters despite the fact that crime, although the largest single element of police work, was only one of a plethora of tasks. At a time of the development of the Police and Magistrates Courts Act, Reiner (1994) describes the home secretary's statement that 'the main job of the police is to catch criminals' as being 'breathtaking in its audacious simple-mindedness'. This simple-mindedness is an issue to which we return again and again in the Home Office's role in this area.

As the decade developed so did the number and scope of targets being set for the service. The new government picked up almost seamlessly from where the previous one left off and initially continued to focus on crime. A major breakthrough for the service was the development of the 'overarching aims and objectives'. This approach finally gave the service a clear mission statement, *'to help secure a safe and just society in which the rights and responsibilities of individuals, families and communities are properly balanced'*. It also gave a value framework in its 'guiding principles'. Whilst the so-called objectives in the model are really only statements of hope or intent, the mechanism overall gives a reasonable description of the breadth and complexity of policing. It was the beginning of an appreciation by the Home Office of the relative position of crime fighting in the police hierarchy of tasks.

By the end of the decade the performance of the service was examined using the following targets and systems:

- The home secretary's priorities: these are thankfully reduced to two, although one of them (to reduce local problems of crime and disorder) is so widely stated that it is of very limited use and only repeats the statutory responsibility the chief constable already has under the Crime and Disorder Act 1998.

- The local targets and objectives set for the force through the local policing plan on an annual basis, the performance of which must be reported and published annually.
- The HMIC and the Audit Commission also monitor, report and publish figures on relative performance in dealing with burglary and violent crime.
- The Audit Commission reports annually on:
  —answering 999 calls
  —incidents requiring immediate response
  —crime and crime detection
  —repeat victimisation
  —road traffic accidents
  —complaints
  —availability of police officers
  —public satisfaction
  —cost
- HMIC also reports on a variety of measures concerning stop and search, racial incidents, traffic offences, sickness absence and gender and ethnic mix of police officers.
- The ACPO report on public satisfaction under a variety of headings including 999 calls, police response to violent crime, burglary, road traffic accidents and perceived levels of foot and mobile patrol, and have also agreed to a target on motor vehicle crime.
- There is a responsibility to report with the CPS on Joint Performance Management of the crime process and a requirement by the Publication of Information (Standards of Performance) Direction, 1996, on letter and telephone answering, buildings open to the public and disability access and information relating to the equal opportunities policy, practices and monitoring.

Out of all of this it is inevitable that there will be measures in one area which actually undermine the effectiveness of the service in another, especially where activities (input), rather than results (outputs and outcomes), are measured. A good example of this is the issue of police visibility. It is accepted that police visibility is an important issue to the public and that high visibility can reduce the fear of crime. However, as is argued in Chapter 2, significant improvements are unlikely in this area without either 20–30,000 more officers or massive changes in systems, processes and practices. It is also firmly established that the patrol function is not particularly effective in crime detection, especially the targeted crimes of burglary, motor vehicle crime and drugs. This meant that any force taking officers away from patrol to improve performance in these other areas through the use of specialist squads, an approach which has a good track record if used properly, would be seen to be failing in this key area of concern to the public (and by logical extension to politicians). The measurement systems are too crude to be able to show the relationship, if there is one, between the two areas, and the public and politicians inevitably focus on the more emotive factor, that is, visibility. Despite this, the Audit Commission insisted on using visibility as a measure of effectiveness. In a similar vein HMIC use the extent of civilianisation as a measure of management effectiveness despite the fact that issues such as changes in pay and conditions of service, operational flexibility and ability to recruit have significantly weakened the case for it and despite the fact that HMIC has recognised this in its own report on value for money. (HMIC 1998)

The introduction of the Best Value regime has now produced a further 30 performance indicators involving 39 individual measures. Out of this there is the proposed efficiency index which, despite all that has been described already about the breadth and complexity of policing, appears to work on the basis that there is that direct causal link between policing inputs and outputs, with the relative efficiency of forces being determined using a Stochastic Frontier Analysis (SFA) approach: I have never come across a more appropriate acronym. Its credibility is based on the fact that it appears to have worked with the newly privatised utilities.

This has happened despite heroic efforts by ACPO to draw the Home Office's attention to the likely outcomes of such a large number of performance indicators and performance regimes. Whilst it is a management truth universally acknowledged that 'what gets measured gets done', there is also the universally acknowledged corollary that measuring everything tends to get nothing done as the organisation knows the quantum of everything but has no idea of the relative value that the measurer wishes to put on anything. The most powerful stakeholder in the police service is the Home Office and its lack of sophistication and competency in dealing with performance management is best demonstrated by the way that the Best Value Performance Indicators (BVPIs) on crime were developed and announced. Somewhere in the heart of its St Anne's Gate HQ, a small team put the initial proposals together. These were then announced with considerable fanfare without the service even being consulted. Put simply the BVPIs were league tables dealing with specific crimes coupled with a requirement that every force should seek to achieve the same performance over time as those in the top 25 per cent. To describe this approach as being simple-minded is to accord it a totally undeserved intellectual depth. For example, robbery was one of the crimes chosen and targets were set in terms of percentage detections and reductions. This meant that some forces with very few robberies were given totally unachievable targets in a crime that was totally irrelevant to the people in that force area. Similarly, forces with higher levels of detections and a low incidence of some crimes, much of which was determined by their demography, set targets for forces with low levels of detections and a high incidence of the same crime, and again significantly determined by demography. Much has been done to recover the situation but that cannot disguise the fact that it happened at all and how clearly it demonstrated the poor grasp the Home Office have on the issue of performance indicators and on performance management overall.

Issues

1. In performance culture 'shared values' is the only way to ensure that integrity is maintained. The leaning of the service towards pragmatism and 'getting the job done' is an unsafe value system for this and must be replaced by one which is more balanced in terms of human rights.
2. The complexity of the police task is such that the absence of a complex, relational database will mean that any focus on particular targets will always skew performance.
3. The general level of performance management skills in the service is too low to support the approach now demanded of it, especially in the areas of problem-solving and statistical and financial analysis.
4. When dealing with deep-seated problems in performance the service must learn to recognise the difference between symptomatic and fundamental solutions and learn to live with the delay necessary to deal with the latter, despite the fact that it is counter-cultural. It is essential that HMIC and the Audit Commission learn the same lesson.
5. The fact that police can act much more quickly than other agencies tends to mean that the service ends up supporting and driving inter-agency projects, often at a disproportionate cost to police. Central and local government should address their decision-making processes to ensure that, when engaged in such projects, their representatives have appropriate delegated authority to commit resources.
6. Every organisation has limited resources and every pound spent on measuring performance cannot be spent on other things. It is thus essential that the measurement systems be limited to, and focused on, those elements that can make a difference. If the Home Office wishes to become involved in the performance regime it must develop the skills necessary to do so and be willing to involve the service as a partner, *rather than* as a mere dogsbody.

Chapter 7: The Management and Governance of the Police

The main parties involved in the management and delivery of policing are, on the police side, the Association of Chief Police Officers (ACPO), the Superintendents' Association, the Police Federation (the Federation) and Unison. Police authorities have their own national association, the Association of Police Authorities (APA) run police forces. Finally, there is the home secretary, the British equivalent of a minister of the interior. As far as police officers are concerned almost all conditions of service are prescribed by statute in various police regulations. The importance of this is that they are negotiated at a national level through the Police Negotiating Board (PNB) by the staff side, mainly composed of the Police Federation and the Superintendents' Association and in some circumstances ACPO, and by the official side, made up of civil servants from the Home Office and representatives from the APA, and in some circumstances ACPO. Once established in regulations there is little room for manoeuvre at a force level.

ACPO

During the period under consideration ACPO suffered badly from the fact that it was never quite sure whether it was an employer, a staff association representing employees, a pressure group or a professional institute. It has now formally separated out the staff association role, with these issues being dealt with by the Chief Police Officers Staff Association (CPOSA) with ACPO becoming a professional institute. However, the fact that the same people are involved in both bodies and that those bodies sometimes need to develop a separate view on the same issues, has led to an uneasy relationship between them. For example, on the subject of the appraisal of chief constables, it was clear that ACPO, whose policy-making process is dominated by chief constables, and CPOSA, which represents all chief officer ranks, took a different view on its practical and constitutional acceptability. In addition, it is not clear that the public are able to differentiate between the two.

It is in its role as an employer that the position of ACPO is least clear. Chief officers have a history of supporting the workforce in the face of criticism, a position which is best exemplified by the approach to the changes in the discipline system. ACPO supported the retention of 'proof beyond reasonable doubt' in discipline cases until it was clear that the Home Office no longer found this tolerable and they were clearly set on changing the system. In almost every other type of employment the burden of proof which is used to decide disciplinary issues is that of the civil court, this being an issue of civil law, i.e. the balance of probabilities. The service has persuaded both the public and politicians that the nature of the job and the exposure to vexatious and malicious complainants is such that the burden of proof should be that of the criminal law, i.e. beyond a reasonable doubt. Until recently ACPO took the same position as the Federation and the Superintendent's Association. (There has been a small, indeed tiny, minority in ACPO, among whom I was one, who advocated the move to the civil standard but it was not able to influence the solid majority for the status quo.)

The fact that ACPO took this stance, however, has enabled the Police Federation to persuade the home secretary that the burden of proof should now be on a sliding scale going from 'balance of probabilities' on less important issues, towards 'beyond reasonable doubt' where the officer's future employment is in question. This means that the service must now struggle with a test that is confused and confusing and which will no doubt only profit lawyers rather than the public. Similarly, in the reaction to the Sheehy inquiry, a number of chief constables openly supported the Federation's position, with one chief constable even sharing the platform at a public protest in Wembley Arena. One outcome of this has been that ACPO has been marginalised in negotiations on police conditions of service, although the situation is improving, probably partly because of the growth of what Reiner describes as professional managers and their gradual replacement of what he described as barons, bobbies and bosses, who had a more paternalistic view of their role vis-à-vis staff.

The major problem that ACPO faces is that of dealing with a rapidly changing environment when there is a need to achieve unanimity on complex issues with 44 chief officers (43 in England and Wales plus the RUC). In recent years ACPO has developed a more coherent and binding process of policy formulation but it is still open to any chief constable to opt out of an ACPO policy provided they declare this. The example of the difficulties that this creates, with the development of the NCS and NCIS, has already been discussed. A number of highly influential chiefs took the view that the service should resist the setting up of these bodies, preferring to retain the regional structure. This led to the creation of two bodies where clearly one would be more sensible and to a long drawn out debate on the issue of primacy of decision-making where the NCS wished to operate in sensitive areas.

ACPO has tried to overcome some of these problems by developing policy through its committees. Whilst this has made a difference and led to quicker policy formulation, it is still very slow and is critically dependent on the skills and focus of the chair. A new, but in future increasing problem for the service, will be the effect of fixed term appointments for chief officers which may mean that it will be difficult to appoint chairs for the desired three-year period within the time available, especially if five-year appointments or contracts become the norm.

In the future the key will be to ensure that the service is able to respond quickly to change and that police officers are involved as key players in the decision-making process. The railway industry and the NHS are stark proof of the fallacy that professional managers can come into complex organisations and run them on the basis of their managerial expertise alone without having to know 'the business'. It is unlikely that the problem will be solved by the institution of a more 'cabinet' style of governance and the appointment of a full-time president of ACPO for a period of three or four years, a proposal currently under discussion. In my view it is inevitable that any such appointee will become closer to the Home Office and further from the service. The effect of the pernicious 'K' factor (a 'promise' of a knighthood or peerage) should not be underestimated. From experience it appears unlikely that 44 chief constables will be willing to give up their authority to an executive president and cabinet and in any case it is highly probable that it is illegal for them to do so as it would constitute an unlawful constraint on their discretion. It is also difficult to make the case vis-à-vis the police authorities and the home secretary for the retention of as much operational autonomy as possible whilst at the same time surrendering that autonomy to an unelected service quango.

Superintendents' Association

The Superintendents' Association now suffers from some of the problems that blighted ACPO in earlier days in that its role as a staff association is somewhat blurred by its aspirations to be considered more as a professional institution when it comes to matters of policy. It was always a fairly marginal contributor in the past, overshadowed by ACPO as far as policy development was concerned and by the Police Federation on issues concerning pay and conditions of service. Just before the election in 1997 it became more influential with the incoming government to the extent that its president was subsequently made a life peer. That influence now appears to have waned and the proposals made at its conference in 2000 were neither innovative nor impactive.

The Police Federation

The Police Federation was set up under statute following the police strike in 1919 on the recommendations of the Desborough committee. The legislation removed the police officer's right to strike or to join a trade union and created the Federation as the staff association that would represent officers between the rank of constable and chief inspector. The Federation rightly makes much of the fact that police officers have fewer civil liberties than the rest of the civilian population as a result of this legislation but it is likely that the threat of a strike is greater than its real potential. The police strike in 1919 was really only effective in Liverpool and that was at a time of universal militancy following the First World War. It is not likely that police officers would have the necessary degree of corporacy to make a strike effective, partly for professional or vocational reasons and partly because of their inherently conservative disposition. Every force has its own independent branch of the Federation and most have between two and four full-time locally elected officers. There are usually good relations between the Federation and chief officers, but this may be due more to the very limited ability that chief officers have to change matters of substance, such as pay and shift patterns, and their historically paternalistic approach, than for any other reason.

Since the 1970s the Federation has proved itself to be a very effective negotiator and propagandist. Its potential in this latter role was recognised by Professor Eric Caines, a member of the Sheehy review board, who correctly anticipated that they would conduct a vocal, vituperative and effective campaign against Sheehy's recommendations to ensure that they were not implemented. Its strength and effectiveness are probably best exemplified by the fact that Home Secretary, Mr Michael Howard, went from a position pre-Sheehy of being a political ' big-hitter ' and potential party leadership contender, to a point some 15 months later, following the adverse publicity that arose from the review's recommendations, where he was barely able to keep his place in cabinet. Another symbol of its strength and a continuous source of annoyance to police leaders is that the media, for a complex range of reasons, usually call on Federation officials to deliver the 'police' view in preference to ACPO, even where the matter under discussion is clearly one requiring senior management knowledge and experience. As a result, they often get a view which supports the rights and privileges of its members rather than one which is representative of the service.

In its negotiating role, although it represents officers from constable to chief inspector, its primary focus is on conditions of service for the constables and sergeants who make up the vast majority of its membership. It has proved to be relatively united over time, although it experiences cyclical difficulties with the Metropolitan Police and forces in the south-east of England when the economic cycle tends to make police pay in these two areas relatively unattractive. Its strength as a negotiator is reinforced by the lack of cohesion on the 'official side' where it faces a group made up of the Association of Police Authorities, civil servants from the Home Office (not famed for their negotiating skills) and, in a more marginal role, ACPO. It has managed in the past to exploit the differences between these parties in order to strengthen its position. For example, the economic cycle issue referred to usually leads to calls for regional pay under some guise or other. The Federation seek to retain a national pay standard and are able to exploit the economic North/South divide where some northern politicians are luke-warm, if not positively hostile to, the idea of officers in the south-east having a higher rate of pay or better conditions of service e.g. housing allowances, than their northern counterparts. The fact that the Federation has one purpose, to protect or enhance its members' conditions of service, means that it can be single-minded in a way that the official side cannot. Thus it can shamelessly use the Metropolitan and south-east officers' relatively poor pay position to lever up national pay and conditions of service.

A final factor, which massively reinforces the Federation's position, is that police conditions of service are not just a written agreement with management, as is the case with most other forms of employment. When agreed they are then promulgated by way of statutory instrument. This is the modern equivalent of writing them in stone. Anything that happens outside of the regulations is not just undesirable, it is unlawful. In addition, since they are very detailed, it is relatively easy to argue from a legalistic viewpoint, that anything not included must be excluded. It does not need much imagination to see how the combination of all of these factors make the negotiation of changed conditions difficult and prolonged. It may have been an appropriate way of working when the pace of change was slow and there were hundreds of forces with the critical need being to ensure uniformity of standards and conditions. It is clearly no longer appropriate to the current need for flexibility and speed of response.

Unison

The situation concerning membership of trade unions by civil staff varies significantly from force to force. My experience is that usually less than 50 per cent of the civil staff will join a trade union, partly because of the fact that they see the police as reasonable employers with relative security of employment, partly because they are spread in small groups around the force which makes organisation more difficult, and partly because they reflect the same conservatism as police officers. The main trade union involved is Unison and it has recently created a section devoted solely to the police. However, it does not appear to be well organised as yet and, although civilians now fill some important operational posts such as call handling and scenes of crime officers, most forces are so organised that they could substitute police officers in these roles relatively quickly. Most pay is negotiated nationally and there are very rarely any industrial disputes.

Police Authorities

Under the Police Act 1964 police authorities were set up comprising one-third magistrates and two-thirds local politicians. The continuing participation of magistrates appears to be an historical anomaly and tends to perpetuate the thinking that the central government (and judges) do not appear to trust local politicians to be impartial and objective in how they manage their local police. This thinking has been perpetuated by the Police and Magistrates Courts Act 1994 which created the single model for police authorities consisting of 17 members, nine of whom are local politicians, three of whom are magistrates nominated from the local bench, and five of whom are independent members, selected by a panel consisting of a police authority and a Home Office nominee. The need for some form of democratic accountability is marginally reflected in the fact that the budget requires the approval of the majority of the elected members; it is marginal in that the police authorities only sets approximately 10 to 20 per cent of the budget, the rest is determined by the Home Office and the Department of the Environment.

In the main, individual chief constables and their police authorities work well in partnership to deliver an efficient and effective policing service. The difficulty arises where there is an irresolvable difference of opinion between them on an issue. In theory if the issue is 'operational' the chief constable has primacy whereas if it is 'policy' it is a matter for the authority. Unfortunately this difference is not at all helpful as most issues can be described as included in either category, e.g. the use of plastic bullets in riot control was thought to be policy by the Northumbria Police Authority which refused to allow the chief constable to purchase them for use in the county. This decision was overruled by the court which declared that the chief constable could use them and that the home secretary, under the royal prerogative, could provide them in the face of the authority's opposition (*R v Secretary of State for the Home Department*, ex parte Northumbria Police Authority, 32 Times Law Reports 19.11.87.) This tension was also exemplified by the running dispute between Lady Margaret Simey, chair of the police authority for Merseyside and Mr Kenneth Oxford, the chief constable, which seemed to last for most of the 1980s, and the differences between a number of chief officers and their authorities on the provision of 'mutual aid' during the Miners' Strike. It is clear that the APA see the authority's historical role as being too limited and they wish to extend its influence, if not power, to direct chief constables. They now look to the Best Value legislation as being the ideal opportunity to achieve this.

The Home Office

Until recently the Home Office fulfilled two roles, one responsible for the police as a whole and the other as the police authority for the Metropolitan Police. The latter changed in 2000 with the establishment of a new police authority for the Metropolitan Police. The fact that the home secretary was the police authority for the Metropolitan Police tended in the past to colour the Home Office's approach to all police problems with the tendency to see them all in a Metropolitan context. For example, the regulations concerning travel and subsistence allowances were only appropriate for a force with an extensive public transport system which is not the reality for most provincial forces; in ethnic minority recruiting the focus was on retention of officers for some considerable time. While this was certainly a problem for the Metropolitan Police, it was not so for all other forces.

Although the Home Office probably has the widest range of responsibility of all ministries, they appear to have a poor appreciation of budgets and of local government organisation and finance which comes under the Department of the Environment. Although partly funded by the Home Office, the police service as it is currently organized, is an integral part of local government. From a police perspective the Home Office always appears to be one step behind either the Treasury (although this appears to be the case for most government departments currently), or the Department of the Environment. For example, the Best Value legislation was appropriate for chief executives of county or unitary authorities, but does not reflect the constitutional position of chief constables. This lack of specific management experience shows through in a number of ways. On budget issues, changes were made in capital and revenue funding in the early 1990s which significantly added to force costs because of their need to lease vehicles where they had previously been purchased outright. More recently in the mismanagement of the Best Value performance indicators, which seemed to reflect either the requirements of the Department of the Environment or a very simple-minded approach to performance management. It has historically kept ACPO out of the discussion loop in pay and conditions of service negotiations, although ACPO's previous close identity with the Federation on employment issues may have had much to do with this.

Summary

In summary, the position as far as the internal governance of the service is concerned is that the people with the major management responsibility for delivering the service do not always have a seat at the negotiating table; those with a guaranteed seat are either civil servants, with no executive responsibility for service delivery, and an association made up of politicians, magistrates and non-elected members, divided by political and North/South loyalties; while the bulk of the workforce is represented by a unified, single minded, well organised and briefed staff association. It is totally unrealistic to expect the paradigm shift described as needed in Chapters 2 and 6 ever to emerge from this process. The whole approach to negotiations is in urgent need of radical review and it is essential that ACPO is enabled to play a role that properly reflects the responsibilities of chief constables and that it, in its turn, participates in the new arrangements clearly and unambiguously as an employer.

The Accountability and Executive Authority of the Chief Constable

The key difference between the police and other central and local government agencies is the executive authority given to chief constables. No other public agency chief has the same level of autonomy. It is not even apparently enjoyed by those in arms-length agencies created by government in the last decade. This executive authority appears to have a strange effect on the mandarins in the Home Office. I am reminded of the description given by my lecturer in jurisprudence of the difference between neurosis and psychosis. A psychotic person knows that two and two make five and he is happy with that knowledge. A neurotic one knows that two and two equals four but cannot live with the knowledge that this is so. They know that the office of chief constable works (e.g. the chief constable is the 'responsible body' in the Crime and Disorder Act), but they cannot always live with all of its consequences. In the Best Value legislation, which was drafted by the Department of the Environment, the chief constable is treated as a chief executive, i.e. someone who can be directed on operational issues by his police authority. There are three reasons why clarity is essential in this area. Firstly, many of the decisions require the professional knowledge that only the chief officer has. Secondly, as discussed in Chapter 4, operational decisions need to be taken quickly and with incomplete information. It is impossible for a committee to do this. Thirdly, the chief constable and not the police authority is held accountable for the outcome of operational decisions and that accountability must be matched with authority.

The difficulties created by such a division in operational responsibility is clearly demonstrated by the position of the governor of Strangeways prison during the riots there in 1990. He was not allowed to make the operational decisions he felt necessary in the circumstances but had to follow instructions from the deputy director general, despite the fact that he had a better overall picture of the situation, knew the prison intimately, was a very senior, experienced and respected governor and, being at the scene, had a better 'feel' for what was, or was not, possible. In the same way the head of the prisons agency appeared to need to accept direction from the Home Secretary on operational issues; that at least is the only conclusion that can be drawn from the infamous Newsnight interview between Mr Michael Howard and Mr Jeremy Paxman. The key issue of the interview was the fact that Mr Howard stated that he only had responsibility for policy and that operational decisions were a matter for the head of the prisons agency. When asked if he had threatened to sack the head of the prisons agency if he did not accept a direction on what was clearly an operational issue, the transfer of a governor, Mr Howard refused to respond, even though the question was put to him some 14 times.

The Common Law

The parameters of the powers and freedoms of a chief constable are not described in statute but have been developed by the common law. In all of the early cases where judges were required to decide who should have the ultimate authority concerning police action and disposition of police resources, the choice was usually between the local authority or the chief constable. In every case the court preferred to give the ultimate authority to the chief constable. The last major case on the issue was that of *R v the Commissioner of Police* ex parte Blackburn (1968). In that case Lord Denning made unequivocal statements concerning the powers and accountability of a chief constable. The most important were:

> . . . *his constitutional status has never been defined by statute or by the court. But I have no hesitation in ordering that, **like every constable in the land***.

(emphasis added) ... *he should be, and is, independent of the executive ... I hold it to be the duty of the Commissioner of Police of the Metropolis, as it is of every chief constable, to enforce the law of the land. He must take steps so as to post his men that crimes may be detected; and that honest citizens may go about their affairs in peace. He must decide whether or not suspected persons are to be prosecuted; and, if need be, bringing the prosecution or see that it is brought.* **But in all these things he is not the servant of anyone, save of the law itself.** (emphasis added). *No Minister of the Crown can tell him that he must, or must not, keep operation on this place or that; or that he must, or must not, prosecute this man or that one. Nor can any police authority tell him so. The responsibility for law enforcement lies on him. He is answerable to the law and to the law alone ...* **it must be for him to decide on the disposition of his force and the concentration of his resources on any particular crime or area.** (emphasis added).

It is clear from this that the court at that time declared the legal status of the chief constable to be one where he had complete freedom in the disposition of the force, both in the offences upon which their efforts would be concentrated and in their geographical location within his force, provided he was taking reasonable steps to enforce the law generally. This autonomy has been reduced by the Police and Magistrates Courts Act 1994 and by the Best Value legislation in the Local Government Act 1998 with the previous clarity being replaced by uncertainty.

The Police Act 1996

The constitutional position was changed initially by the Police and Magistrates' Courts Act 1994 whose relevant provisions have now been incorporated in the Police Act 1996. The significant changes in the constitutional position of the chief constable are found in Sections 7, 8, 10 (the requirement to draw up a policing plan for the area) and 11 (the power to require to resign) of the 1996 Act. Under the former the chief constable must be consulted before the police authority sets its objectives; he has the responsibility for drawing up the draft of the local policing plan but need only 'pay due regard to the final plan in carrying out his responsibilities' under Section 8 and 10. However, the combination of the changes mean that the power under Section 11 (2) has teeth for the first time in that it creates an effective framework to measure objectively the efficiency and effectiveness of the chief constable in the day-to-day running of the force by their ability to deliver the agreed policing plan.

Section 38 of the Act gives the home secretary the power to establish objectives and, more importantly, gives him the power to establish performance targets. Assurances were given at the time that it would not be used to set 'hard' targets for individual forces. However, the language of the section allows this and, in this way, it has a significant potential to direct resources, especially in the light of the power in Section 11 to get rid of the chief constable if they fail to run the force in an efficient and effective way. It is clear from the performance regime under which the service now labours that these 'hard' targets have now been set, whether or not the home secretary wishes to hold the chief constable or the police authority to account under this particular section. There is a powerful lesson here on how little value such assurances have and how little subsequent home secretaries feel bound by them.

It can be seen from this that the powers of a chief constable as described by Lord Denning have been significantly changed. The policing plan clearly causes the chief constable to focus resources both in terms of offences and in terms of geographical cover. The existence of the policing plan means that the office no longer has that autonomy described by Lord Denning, and there is a system of accountability which can enforce compliance with that plan.

Best Value

Best Value builds on the changes initiated by the Police and Magistrates Courts Act in that the responsibility for the performance plan is placed unambiguously on the police authority and not the chief constable. The Home Secretary retains powers of inspection, review and target setting. The way in which this cuts across the traditional operational autonomy of the chief constable has already been discussed. The significant change is that it creates an absolute responsibility on the police authority for obtaining Best Value. The previous legislation recognised the chief constable's operational autonomy, albeit creating a new context in which it would be exercised. The difficulty that this creates is that there can now arise situations in which responsibility is unclear. It is ironic that while this has been happening, the same government has been trying to create for headmasters exactly that form of autonomy currently enjoyed by chief constables. In this, those responsible for education policy clearly recognise the fact that a clear devolution of a single line budget, together with the power to use it and be accountable for it, would logically lead to improvements in performance, while those in the Home Office continue to labour under the neurosis already described.

In the service the situation can now arise where one element of the law gives responsibility to the chief constable while at the same time the Best Value legislation gives an overriding authority to the police authority. For example, in law the chief constable is treated as the employer for all police officers and is personally responsible for ensuring safe systems of work. If the police authority decided that Best Value in vehicle fleet management could be achieved by using a vehicle marking system which was cheaper but less effective than that which the chief constable would prefer, it is not clear against whom the officer should take legal action should they suffer an injury in which vehicle marking was believed to be a contributory factor.

The Office of Constable

It is clear that these legislative changes have significantly changed the constitutional position of the chief constable as described by Lord Denning in those matters concerning the general disposition of the force; policy issues; which type or categories of offences will be prosecuted and how. Under the Best Value legislation this may even now extend to everyday policing issues. It does not appear to affect the individual constable's right to pursue, or not, any particular case. This discretion appears to arise out of the fact that the status of the constable in common law is that of an officer of the Crown and not an employee (there is no case law exactly on the issue and the declarations on it have only been as part of other decisions). The importance of this issue is that the chief constable's autonomy also arises out of the discretion that the law bestows on the office of constable and how that discretion is exercised in the chief officer role. Any change in the constitutional position of the constable must therefore be reflected in that of the chief constable.

This may now have been changed by recent health and safety legislation. Under Section 1 of the Act of 1997 anyone who holds the office of constable shall be 'treated as an employee' of the relevant officer. The 'relevant officer' in the generality of cases means the chief constable. Here the constable is described as an employee for the first time in statute; and every chief is also a constable. It is accepted that the description is strictly limited in the statute to issues of health and safety and is only 'for the purposes of this part (of the Act)'.

While the service will be reassured by the government that there is no intention to expand this interpretation, attention must be paid to what has happened in the past elsewhere concerning another government agency i.e. the prison service. In 1994 prison officers were engaged in industrial action because of the overcrowding of prisons. In the course of this action the Prisons Agency successfully had an injunction issued against prison officers, preventing them from striking or inciting others to strike on the basis that in the Prison Act they had been given some of the powers of a constable inside prisons. The judge in the case stated that with the power came the corresponding responsibilities. They were thus proscribed from striking by the same legislation that prevented constables from striking and being incited to strike. The Prison Officers Association did not try to reverse this ruling but tried to put it in a different context in order to achieve their objective i.e. to close prisons, in subsequent cases. They were also unsuccessful in this approach. The important issue is that they did not appear to believe that it was worthwhile appealing the District Court judge's opinion to either the Court of Appeal or the House of Lords. The judge's finding has now been written into statute in the Criminal Justice and Public Order Act (1994).

The lesson from this is clear. Legislation is a bit like a missile without a guidance system. Once it is launched its originators have no prescriptive control over its subsequent use. The two key pillars that supported the traditional view of the chief officer's position in the constitution have been changed; one has been changed significantly in order to improve accountability. That matter has been fully debated and is essentially one for Parliament which has made its will clear. It is the service's responsibility to comply and, within the legislation, to provide the best service possible to the community. The potential change brought about by the health and safety legislation, combined with that concerning Best Value, has not been subject to the same scrutiny.

Conclusion

Both the Police and Magistrates Court and the Crime and Disorder Acts made specific provision for the operational autonomy of the chief constable. The argument for doing the same in the Local Government Act was ignored and chief constables are treated in it as if the office was the same as that of a local government chief executive. The home secretary has made a commitment, outside of statute, to ensure that the operational autonomy of chief officers is not affected. Unlike statute, such assurances are not binding on either the home secretary or his successors. The position of the tri-partite arrangement is now somewhat akin to that of the cartoon character who walks away from the cliff edge believing that the ground is still there; it is only when he looks down that he finds the perilous nature of his position, fractions of a second before plummeting into the depths.

This combination of factors may now mean that in another situation like that of the Miners' Strike in the 1980s, the chief constable will no longer be able to make a commitment to support other forces without the express consent of the police authority or in the face of its disapproval. These situations by their very nature require the commitment of significant resources and are bound to endanger the authority's Best Value programme.

If the issue is one which has polarised the positions of the two parties and one is in government while the other dominates local government, central government may find that chief constables can no longer lawfully provide them with that level of support that they have always taken for granted in the past. What is clear is that there is a justiciable issue which may be of sufficient weight to persuade a judge to grant an interim injunction supporting the authority. This would be enough to deprive government of the services of the force or forces at the time of critical need. Everyone should bear in mind that, at the time of the Miners' Strike in the 1980s, the Labour Party looked no more capable of returning to government than do the Conservatives in 2001. Their current drive to change the office of chief constable to one resembling that of any other government agency chief executive may not suit them in all circumstances.

These arrangements have emerged without critical examination, as if the position of the three parties had remained unchanged. Given the significant changes which have been made in the legislation and the lack of clarity concerning the respective positions of the parties under the law, it would surely be preferable to have that debate now rather than wait until a situation of breakdown has occurred, such that one or other of the parties feels the need to seek a judicial decision on the issue. It is a political decision and should be made openly following a robust debate, rather than leaving the judiciary with the unenviable task of gleaning a sensible conclusion from what has become a morass of counter-indicators of political intention.

Issues

1. The current pay and conditions of service arrangements cannot deliver the nature and scale of change needed to take the service forward into the 21st century. There is an urgent need to create a body on the official side that has the same coherence and focus of purpose as the Police Federation, and to a lesser extent the Superintendents' Association. ACPO must be a key member of this body and play a full part as an employer.
2. As long as there are 44 chief constables it does not seem possible to obtain the speed and corporacy of decision-making needed. A cabinet arrangement and full-time president, while streamlining the process, do not sit easily in either legal or practical terms, with the concept of autonomy and operational independence.
3. Police authorities as presently constituted fall between the stools of democratic accountability and quangos made up of people selected by government on their potential to contribute. In larger forces the

'democratic link' is very thin and any move to amalgamate the smaller forces will significantly weaken their already tenuous links.

4. The changes in the constitutional position of both the chief constable and the police authorities has significantly changed the balance of power between the service, as represented by them, from them to the Home Office. This has been done in a piecemeal, confused way leaving the current position of all of the parties uncertain.

5. The independence of the office of chief constable, around which much of what is admired about the British police service hangs, now exists as a matter of convention and not of law. Convention may be used to help interpret law, it cannot overrule a specific legal provision. There is a need for an open and informed debate on this key issue and for the political decision made on its future to be reflected in statute.

Chapter 8: Structure

Force Structure

The British police force model is one based on geography upon which certain functional specialisms are overlaid. It starts at constable level where the ground is divided into a number of beats or neighbourhoods, which are the responsibility of one officer, usually carrying some designation such as permanent beat officer, home beat officer or beat manager. As described in Chapter 2 this officer is usually expected to perform a problem-solving role dealing with longer-term issues. In a number of forces it is sadly the ideal rather than the reality. A number of these beats are then usually gathered together and are made the responsibility of a patrol car. This is the theory, it is not always supported by the subsequent deployment reality. The primary operational unit is usually called a Basic Command Unit (BCU). In rural areas this will usually be made up of a number of smaller stations, each headed by an inspector or chief inspector, and in larger conurbations there will be one or maybe two police stations responsible for the whole area. This unit is responsible for 90-95 per cent of policing in the area and is usually under the command of a superintendent or chief superintendent. When the Audit Commission initially proposed the concept the ideal number was reckoned to be between 150 and 200 police officers. By the late 1990s the ideal number had become, for most forces, between 250 and 350 police officers. Some forces have BCUs of over 400 officers and at least one force has BCUs of around 1,000 . In my view the latter are unsustainable over time due to the internal span of control and the external political demands. They will eventually break down into smaller units, either by deliberate decision or in operational practice (but that is an argument for another day). What is significant is how quickly the consensus on an 'ideal' number broke down.

On top of the BCU is overlaid a large number of functional specialisms. These will include administration and support functions such as a vehicle fleet management, ICT provision and support, finance, personnel, scientific services, training, organisational development, specialist CID, operational support in the form of support groups and armed response, traffic police and call handling and deployment. While the pattern is not exactly the same in every force, differences will be at the margin, usually determined by the availability of suitable buildings and the general demography of the force.

Current Structure

The proposition that there is a relationship between the size and efficiency of forces has underpinned the gradual amalgamation of forces since the end of the Second World War. In the 1950s there was a gradual absorption of small borough forces by county forces. This culminated in the main in the early 1960s, following the implementation of the Royal Commission on the Police recommendations. This determined that the lowest number for viability was around 500. This number gradually grew to around 1,000 by the end of that decade. It is not clear what evidence, if any, was used to substantiate the viability of either number, nor of the nature of research which was carried out pre- or post-amalgamation which demonstrated any clear performance advantage gained from the changes, although the 1,000 officer standard has proved to be very resilient.

The next period of major change followed local government reorganisation in the early 1970s which created the large metropolitan authorities. When these were abolished it was decided that the police forces created should remain, presumably on the basis of efficiency and the difficulty and costs of breaking them up again. There have been no further amalgamations since that time. At present over half the forces in England and Wales have less than 2,000 police officers, there being another significant band of forces between 2,000 and 3,500, with a final top grouping of between 5,000 and 7,000. It is ironic that, although civilianisation has been greatly encouraged by government and HMIC and has led to civilians filling a significant number of key operational posts, when police establishments are discussed they are always, very insultingly, ignored. It also demonstrates the nonsense of a 'magical' number for viability in that an element of the service, which makes up nearly one-third of its total, is usually ignored in the debate.

The current structure has five basic types of force. They are:

1. Forces based on large conurbations or groups of conurbations, e.g. Greater Manchester, West Midlands (former Metropolitan authority forces).
2. Forces incorporating more than two counties, e.g. Thames Valley, West Mercia.
3. Joint authorities of two counties, e.g. East and West Sussex, Devon and Cornwall.
4. Larger forces based on a single county, e.g. Kent, Hampshire, Essex.

5. Smaller forces based on a single county, e.g. Warwickshire, Northamptonshire, Derbyshire.

The major difficulty faced by those who would advocate amalgamations rather than the status quo or a move to a regional or national force is that of deciding the criteria by which the selection for amalgamation should be made. The usual approach is the simple one of determining a number below which forces are not felt to be sustainable. As described above this is difficult to prove in empirical terms and is usually done as a matter of judgement, however that is defined, by some person or organisation on which the government places reliance e.g. HMCIC's estimate of 3,500 in the early 1990s. Given the scale of disruption that would ensue, this does not appear to be a particularly attractive approach unless there are clear and obvious grounds to show that the change will result in an improved service to the public. If the figure, on police numbers, was taken to be 1,000 it would only affect two forces. The next step up is probably 1,500; this would affect about 25 per cent of forces. The next step is probably 2,000; this would affect over half of the forces in England and Wales. Loughborough University's research on the relative efficiency of forces indicated that the optimum size was between 1,500 and 4,500. Apart from the fact that this is too wide a band to be helpful, it is difficult to take too seriously a research study which uses clear-up rates, traffic prosecutions and breathalysers as the main productivity measures. Like a number of others it identified that there were a large number of relevant indicators but since they were too difficult to measure it chose to ignore them, i.e. measuring what was easy rather than what was relevant.

At the time of the last major debate on this issue in the early 1990s, when the then HMCIC suggested that the 'ideal' size for any force was around 3,500, some work was done on the relative efficiency and effectiveness of larger and smaller forces. In the main this looked at cost and crime in very crude terms, i.e. the cost per officer or per head of population, the overall crime rate and crime detection rates. These are not good indicators of overall efficiency or cost effectiveness for a number of reasons, the main one being that like is not being compared with like. It is nonsensical to compare the cost per officer or per head of population for policing Handsworth in the West Midlands with that of policing Carmarthen in rural South Wales or even with a moderately large county town such as Norwich. The calls on police in areas of high social deprivation and high-density housing are always significantly higher and there are very few drugs gangs with their associated turf wars in Carmarthen or Norwich. In the same way the crime profile will also be significantly different, with the 'degree of difficulty' faced by a larger force being significantly greater than that facing the smaller one.

There can be exceptions to this rule. Bedfordshire has a complex community mix, with the highest proportion of members of ethnic minority communities outside of the metropolitan areas, a high level of social deprivation for a south-eastern county and with an unusually serious problem of violent crime. However, even here, most of the crime is local, i.e. committed by people local to the neighbourhood and thus likely to be known to the police, and the 'degree of difficulty' is still less than that faced by West Midlands or Greater Manchester where 'local' has a much wider connotation. In this type of comparison the large forces will always come second. An (unpublished) study carried out in forces in the south-east of England did show that the smaller forces appear to have lower proportionate costs running some central functions such as finance and ICT. While this may call into question the contention that the mere amalgamation of forces will lead to reduced costs through economies of scale in supporting some central functions, the study did not cover either the quality or range of services offered which may have changed the picture quite dramatically.

It is possible to compare models in a number of key characteristics to establish the potential relative efficiency of each:

- economies of scale
- management flexibility
- operational flexibility
- accountability
- representation

Economies of Scale

It goes without saying that the larger the organisation the more likely it is that economies of scale can be made. However, care must be taken in assuming that economies of scale are possible merely by increasing the size of the organisation. If much of the function is routine and labour-intensive, it is unlikely that increasing the size of the organisation will necessarily of itself produce any worthwhile economies. For example, in policing, larger forces will not produce economies of scale in the patrol function itself, although it may enable some economies to be made in the support services for it. In the same way much of the routine administration which is done within the service, such as routine record maintenance, the kind of inquiry made by both the recruiting branches and prosecutions departments, are all fairly labour-intensive and gathering them together in a larger organisation would only produce marginal cost savings in their management and housing costs. There are, however, three areas in which there can be significant savings made from economies of scale in policing. They are senior command, research and development and ICT.

Senior command

Most forces have a command team made up of a chief constable, deputy chief constable, a number of assistant chief constables, varying from one to five depending on the size of the force, a director each of finance, personnel and ICT. In the smaller forces it is more usual for the personnel and ICT heads to be subordinate to one of the ACCs. Using the eastern ACPO region as an example, there are currently six chief constables, six deputy chief constables, nine assistant chief constables, six directors each of finance, personnel and ICT. If this became a regional force it would have a total of approximately 10,000 police officers and 5,000 civilians. A suggested top team for such a region would consist of one chief constable, a deputy chief constable, four assistant chief constables, one director each of finance, personnel and ICT; a total of nine chief officers. Taking the support these chief officer teams have such as staff officers, drivers, PAs etc, this would produce a saving of approximately £3 million; taken nationally it would produce savings of approximately £25 million.

Research and development

Every force has some research and development capability. The growth of the use of performance management, the development of more sophisticated analytical and intelligence techniques, the need for strategic planning to service the force, the police authority, the HMIC, the Audit Commission and the Home Office, the growing bureaucratic challenge presented by Best Value, all have led to a significant growth in this area and a consequent significant investment by forces in it. If regional forces were created this would lead to savings of around £8 million. This would not be the only saving however, as there would also be a significant improvement in the quality of work done because the larger teams would enable the recruitment of more highly qualified personnel and a significant reduction in the duplication of effort. The smaller number of forces should lead to easier consensus on the part of chief constables and may make them more confident in allowing one regional team to take the lead on a particular issue, further reducing duplication and perhaps enhancing both speed of development and quality of product.

Information and Communication Technology (ICT)

To paraphrase Mark Twain, there are liars, damn liars and ICT sales people. ICT companies have turned over-promising and under-delivering, to the police service at least, into an art form. Looking at the experience of the Immigration Department and the London Ambulance Service, the other public services have the same problem. ICT in the police is a weary tale of the conceptual nirvana of systems design, followed by the actual hell of systems implementation, the long-time purgatory of online system development and improvement which leads to a point where, just as the pain has stopped and the system has begun to function effectively, it is declared out of date and in the industry terms 'no longer commercially supportable', whence the merry-go-round begins again. The massive improvements in processing power and communications technology, which have come about in the last five years and will come about more and more quickly into the future, present an enormous opportunity for the service in that it is now possible to set up single systems to serve the whole of England and Wales. The system can be located, serviced and maintained in one centre while its access is distributed nationally. The Police National Computer (PNC) and the automated fingerprint recognition system (AFR) show only too clearly what could be achieved if the service could develop a more co-ordinated and coherent approach in this key area.

The history of ICT in the police is an inevitable consequence of the fact that there are 43 police forces, each with different budgetary provisions, each with different levels of knowledge and expertise in ICT at senior command level, and each with the burden of a number of legacy systems which come up for replacement at different times. The lack of willingness by the Home Office to take up the burden of leadership in this area has led to the rather piecemeal development of major systems which use different data and operating standards and which have extreme difficulty in exchanging information. The exception has been the major inquiry system, the Home Office Large and Major Enquiry System (HOLMES), which began its development in the early 1980s and which now enables forces to link such inquiries fairly effectively. Even this system, which was led by the Home Office, exemplifies the lack of leadership given by them. Their refusal to restrict its provision to one supplier led to forces acquiring systems that were still incapable of full integration up until the early 1990s. The service was put in the ludicrous situation of having a system which was theoretically integratable but in which a reliable exchange of information could only be achieved by each force engaged in a major inquiry running its system separately and 'hard-wiring' any other force engaged in the same inquiry into each other's incident room (i.e. setting up a dedicated telephone link between the two rooms so that each had direct access into the other's system). This meant that if the forces were engaged in the same inquiry but had a system supplied by a different manufacturer, (even at one time a different model by the same manufacturer), each would need to run a separate database but would provide the other's incident room with a terminal and access. Thus each incident room had to check and update the other's database physically rather than have the technology to carry out the task for which it was designed.

In the early 1990s ACPO developed an ICT strategy but it was doomed to fail as it focused on system procurement. The difficulty here is that those forces which had already developed the use of ICT were all at different points of development e.g. at the time Thames Valley was procuring its first command and control system, Bedfordshire was replacing one. Given the fact that it takes approximately two years to develop a system and at least a year, depending on how robust the system supplier's project management has been, to implement it, those forces already engaged in the implementation of an ICT strategy were unwilling to wait for other forces to catch up. In addition, the long period which seems inevitably to follow on between the system's development and its eventual rollout to the whole of the service, made it appear unattractive to those nominated to receive the system last, as they would enjoy a much shorter system lifespan. A better approach would have been to agree on the data standards for those key elements of data in which information exchange was essential and make that a part of the procurement requirement to the company supplying the system. The growing frustration with the unwillingness of the Home Office to lead and the need to create an ability to deliver national systems quickly led ACPO to propose the setting up of a national agency to achieve this: the Police Information Technology Organisation (PITO). This however has turned out to be a poor reward for the service's corporacy, as it has become more subservient to the Home Office than the needs of the service and the first round of systems procurement under its direction has proved to be highly unsatisfactory. The performance of PITO to date demonstrates the needs for the procurement body to be directed by the service itself, and for those with knowledge of the business and the responsibility for delivering the results having ownership and direction of this key tool for performance improvement and enhancement.

If the three factors are considered in the light of a proposal for amalgamation as opposed to one for regional forces, it can be seen that the gains which can be made in senior command and research and development must necessarily be significantly smaller since they will release significantly fewer posts; the closer the proposed structure is to the status quo, the lower the level of saving. Amalgamation would not serve the needs of ICT as it would not create an organisation that was big enough to displace PITO and the Home Office.

Management Flexibility

A larger organisation gives significantly more flexibility in terms of recruitment, training, selection and retention of staff. Staff costs make up approximately 80 per cent of police budgets. If there are budget reductions of any size it is inevitable that they will be reflected in staff numbers. Under current regulations it is impossible to make police officers redundant so the full burden of redundancy must fall on the civil staff. However redundancy is a very crude tool for reducing staff numbers for two reasons. Firstly, it is necessary to make additional payments to the staff made redundant, which means that it is very difficult to recover the full costs in any one financial year. Secondly, it is necessary to go through a fairly complicated process to create redundancies, which causes significant staff morale problems and tends to put a blight on staff development and commitment while it is going on. Since redundancy is not an option for police officers, the only way to control their numbers is through recruitment. In the smaller forces this can mean that there are recruiting freezes for six months to over a year. This then has consequences elsewhere as the force usually retains a recruitment and training capability that is underused during this period. The larger the force the better able it is to flatten out the peaks and troughs of the cycle and, having a larger budget, the better it is able to deal with budget cuts.

In training the larger force can offer a more complete range of training internally. This is more cost-effective as it can be tailor-made to fit the needs of the force, can be brought on stream and discontinued more quickly and can usually be done without the need for residential training that massively increases the overall cost. It is a significant failing of National Police Training (NPT) that it takes one to three years to change any particular element. The more complex the training area the more bodies are involved; for some this can mean the Home Office, the APA, ACPO, NPT, the Superintendents' Association, and the Federation. Too often, because consensus is an issue, it becomes the lowest common denominator rather than best possible practice.

The same applies to selection and retention. The larger force is able to offer a fuller range of career choice and can usually sustain selection for both promoted posts and specialist posts more consistently than the smaller forces, thus enabling it to retain its better officers. In smaller forces when there is a slowing down of movement, the better and more ambitious officers are tempted to apply to other forces. In all these factors clearly the larger the force the more benefits there are.

Elsewhere I advocate the need to consider direct entry, either directly into specialisms such as CID or one of its sub-sets e.g. fraud, or at inspector or superintendent ranks. The smaller forces would find it much more difficult and relatively more expensive to set up and manage the recruitment and selection process for this proposal. It is also likely to be significantly more difficult to introduce direct entrants to police work where the specialist numbers themselves are small, e.g. if the force fraud squad only has three or four officers, the introduction of a new officer under this process would be difficult and relatively expensive to do. In addition a change of this magnitude is certain to cause enormous, deep-seated resentment and those joining under it would need considerable support and protection, to begin with at least. The experience of the Trenchard scheme in the 1930s and the firm stance that the Federation and Superintendents' Association have taken whenever it is raised are powerful indicators of this.

A consistent complaint from communities about the police is the lack of continuity caused by officer movements. This is true of every level up to the chief constable. Local communities complain that they no sooner get to know a beat manager or permanent beat officer than they move on. The same is true of inspectors running small stations and more critically of chief superintendents in charge of BCUs. The latter are the main service delivery vehicles and most forces have attempted, as far as is possible, to ensure that they have a co-terminus border with the local political unit or units. The best relationship is usually found where a BCU is co-terminus with a unitary authority. In the regional police force model the number of chief officer posts would be dramatically reduced, as would the number of senior staff functions in the various headquarters. This would significantly reduce the number of promotions open to the chief superintendent ranks and would necessarily slow down the whole promotion system. A significant benefit from this would be an ability to post the more able officers to the BCU for a much longer period of time, ideally three to five years. In addition, because of the number and range of posts available, the chief constable could make commitments to the senior superintendents, which they could have some expectation that they could live up to.

In order for the model to be complete it would be essential that the retirement provisions for senior officers be reviewed. The current position is that a chief superintendent can retire as soon as they have achieved 30 years service. If they joined at the earliest possible age this can mean retiring at the age of 48. For chief officer ranks retirement is available as soon as the officer has achieved 30 years service and is over the age of 55 or has completed their fixed appointment. This can mean that the chief officer can retire in their early fifties. Officers who choose not to retire are effectively choosing to work for approximately 25 per cent of their salary since they are entitled to 66 per cent on pension and will stop paying 11 per cent into the pension fund. It is not possible under current regulations for the police authority to change any of these factors. Dramatic changes must be made in the pension provision so as to make it at least cost neutral for officers to remain in service after their earliest retirement point if any continuity is to be achieved and the expert knowledge which these officers have accumulated over time is to be retained. It is essential that superintendents and chief officers are dealt with together as the current situation arose from the fact that they were dealt with differently. It used to be the case that the earliest retirement age for a chief officer was 60 and only then with the agreement of their police authority. It was noticed that a significant number of able chief superintendents were not applying for the Senior Command Course, and thus ACPO rank, as they preferred the option of retiring at 49. The retirement age for ACPO was then reduced to 55 as of right. It was further reduced to the end of the fixed appointment following their introduction.

Operational Flexibility

The case for larger forces giving greater operational flexibility is very clear. Among the problems for the service already dealt with in Chapter 5 concerning organised crime, are the issues of cross-border crime. These are the crimes of middle level drug dealing, ram-raiding and lorry hi-jacking. To these can be added the paedophile rings which are now a national and international problem. In addition, the growing extremism of the animal rights movement creates significant problems for smaller forces, both in terms of the difficulty in containing the protesters and in developing and sharing intelligence. Finally, there is the issue of serial crimes at the more serious end of the scale e.g. murder and rape. These will more often than not involve more than one force, with the consequent difficulties in determining which force has primacy, and dividing costs and effort.

In addition to this there are now a significant number of specialisms that benefit from the larger scale. Whilst most forces have entered into consortia or bilateral agreements in order to provide some of them, there are still significant gaps which can often only be made up by specifically contracting in the service. As far as air cover is concerned, most forces have joined a consortium of some sort; however the current size of consortia has not created the ideal flexibility e.g. most consortia have access to one or two helicopters whereas the ideal would have a larger number of helicopters and would include some fixed wing provision. Specialist services such as mounted police and diving units are very expensive to maintain and can only be afforded by the larger forces. This means that when the smaller forces have an operational requirement for their use they are critically dependent on the owning force not having a requirement to use them at the same time. In the CID, larger forces would create a more coherent and co-ordinated intelligence and forensic science service. It would also provide a more solid basis for surveillance teams and other specialist CID functions such as drug and fraud squads, and financial tracking units whose use is bound to grow following the recent changes in legislation.

The containment of disorder is a continuing theme for the police service and public order training is now a very expensive requirement both because of the need to deal with disorder effectively using minimum force and because of the health and safety requirements for officer protection. Larger forces would enable both of these factors to be dealt with more cost effectively since it would be possible to train a smaller number of officers to a higher level of expertise.

Accountability

As already described the police service does not appear to be modelled on any consistent theme given the range of sizes and the different ways in which the service is organised. However, compared to the way in which local government is organised in England, the police service is a model of congruity and cohesion. Following reorganisation in the early 1990s, local government is now organised on either a unitary or county and district basis. However, even here, the differences are more than significant, they are actually counter-productive. The unitary authorities range from those which are large enough to provide all of the services with which they are entrusted through to some so small that they have difficulty in doing so. In the same way some counties which should have been made unitary have actually ended up with an expensive and costly form of local government.

To use Bedfordshire as an example, it is a county of just over 500,000 people. Before reorganisation it consisted of the county council and four district councils. It has the reasonably large conurbation made up of Luton and Dunstable in the south, the middle sized county town of Bedford in the north and a scattering of smaller towns spread through the centre. If all historical considerations are put to one side, the logical geopolitical division of the county would be into the Luton and Dunstable conurbation of approximately 200,000, and the rest of the county of 300,000. The resultant unitary authorities would be big enough to be self-sustaining and could comfortably deliver all of the services required at a local level. Instead of this Luton was established as a unitary authority and the rest of the county was organised on three districts under the umbrella of the county council. One of the districts, mid-Bedfordshire, is a completely artificial construction with two small centres of population, one of which has stronger connections with

Cambridgeshire than the town housing the district council offices. This means that the population of Bedfordshire pays for five authorities where two would more than suffice and that the conurbation of Luton and Dunstable is artificially split. It makes the co-ordinated approach required by the Crime and Disorder Act much harder to achieve both in co-ordinating the work of all of the authorities and, crucially, because the budget has been split four ways rather than one and needs to carry a larger management and bureaucratic overhead, there is less tax payers' money left to fund projects that can make a difference.

As already stated most of the issues which underpin crime prevention and reduction at a strategic level are matters for local or national government agencies and not for the police e.g. drugs rehabilitation, education and situational crime prevention. In my experience policing works best where there is a clear link between the BCU and the local political unit. All of this points to reorganising local government on a template of population groupings of 2–300,000 people. It is likely that this would succeed in most of the country outside of the major conurbations of Merseyside, Manchester and Birmingham, although even here it is possible to break the cities down into clearly identifiable neighbourhoods or groups of neighbourhoods to form units of this size.

The shape of local government is critical to the successful reorganisation of the police service. It is important to remember that the last police reorganisation that took place in 1974 created new forces, which were clearly aligned with other local government provision. The abolition of the Metropolitan authorities broke down that relationship and the mess, which was the result of the local government reorganisation in the early 1990s, did the same to the rest of the country. Unless there is to be a massive democratic deficit it is essential that the police service is so structured that it has a clear relationship with local government. To establish a regional police force without a regional government would be to create a national force with little in the way of local accountability. However, if there were a regional government that was underpinned by large unitary local authorities there could be a parallel and equal organisation of the police service into large self-sustaining BCUs, organised under a regional head. In this form of organisation it would be possible to create a more local accountability between the BCU commander and the local government unit. It would be possible to reinforce this through various stratagems such as the involvement of the local government politicians in the selection of their BCU commander and in using taxation raised by the local government unit to partially fund its local BCU. It is unlikely that this would be 100 per cent funding but it could certainly be sustained at least at the current level of 10 to 20 per cent. It is essential, if the accountability is to be real and not cosmetic, that the local government unit has some ability to shape the style and content of local policing.

The same case can be made for a reform of local government, so that it is organised in larger self-sufficient units that are capable of delivering all local government services if the concept of a regional police force is rejected in favour of a number of amalgamations. The organisation of the police into large, highly devolved BCUs would thus allow large amalgamated forces to better reflect local opinion and to better relate to and co-ordinate with other local services. There is already a democratic deficit in the management of policing in that eight out of seventeen members of the police authority are not elected but nominated. In the larger county and joint authority forces this means that some authorities are not represented at all as it is necessary to balance the party 'mix' in the nine elected members. The extension of larger forces without reform of local government or the constitution of police authorities will further increase this deficit.

Chief Officer Representation

As already discussed it has proved to be difficult to achieve consensus in ACPO in some key decisions in the past and doing so is usually a long and sometimes tortuous process. It is difficult to see how it could be other with the need to persuade 44 chiefs of different ages and with different styles of both management and policing who are influenced by their local issues. The proposal to have a full-time president and a form of cabinet governance will doubtlessly help to speed up the process and enable ACPO to respond quickly to issues as they arise, rather than allow the Federation to do so, as is too often the case at present. There still remains however the constitutional independence of each chief constable and the new arrangements will not assist where there is a real deep-seated issue of difference, e.g. as was the case with the establishment of the NCS.

A regionally based service would have a much smaller number of chief officers. This could have a significant number of benefits. Consensus would be easier and quicker to achieve. The resulting forces would be big enough to balance the 'Met' effect discussed earlier and the chief constables could expect the same access to ministers and senior civil servants as is currently enjoyed by the commissioner, thus enabling the service to present a more balanced view of policing to government. It would be possible to ensure that people who really understood 'the business' would be represented at the highest level rather than on the ad hoc and 'grace and favour' basis which is all too often the current position e.g. the difficulty the service has in being represented on the group which is developing an ICT strategy for the criminal justice system where the police, the sole entry point for everything that happens subsequently, are not seen as important enough for inclusion. None of these would be achieved by amalgamations, especially at the 'tinkering' end of that spectrum.

A final thought on this issue is the whole question of leadership: a matter currently under debate by ACPO, the APA and the Home Office. I believe that the leadership provided by ACPO at its best is at least as good, if not in the main better, than that provided in any other government body, and in that I include the armed services, the civil service and local government. As I write I am daily confronted on the news programmes by the debacle of the Ministry of Agriculture and Fisheries, the Cabinet Office and the army trying to get to grips with the foot and mouth epidemic. Some eight weeks into the problem they cannot produce reliable information on their key performance indicator, the number of newly discovered cases being slaughtered within 24 hours; they are digging up cattle for fear of allowing BSE into the water system; lambs are dying in awful conditions in the fields because the bureaucracy cannot deal quickly enough with requests for local movements; there is a fear that trucks used for carrying slaughtered animals are also being used to carry animal feed. The experience of 34 years tell me that if the service was in charge and this was going on, the newspapers would be full of criticism from 'informed sources close to the minister', if not public ministerial condemnation on our leadership. In fact the 'can do' culture of the service is a major strength and there are very few major incidents where it has failed to deliver. That said, it is fair to ask whether an organisation with a single entry point, at its lowest level, can consistently produce such a large number of chief officers or whether it is better to reduce the number radically, establish the service ceiling for the majority at chief superintendent (a rank that would be a mini chief constable following the devolution of budgets and authority) allowing only the very best to achieve chief officer rank.

Europe

A final reason to consider regional forces is the European dimension. Britain is one of the few countries in Europe that does not have a national force. Most European forces are organised, like their legal systems, on a Napoleonic code basis as a part of the ministry of justice or as a gendarmerie as part of the ministry of defence. The role and constitutional position of the constable and chief constable do not fit easily into the European construct of policing and criminal process where the judiciary tends to play a much more dominant role. European countries are however usually organised on a 'province' (no matter how described) basis and the re-organisation of the service regionally would fit easily into this model thus allowing for more effective bi-lateral relations with other European forces on a case-by-case basis. It would also guarantee a level of workload which would make permanent liaison workable, develop the legal and systems expertise needed to be effective in this complex area and establish the personal connections essential to effective working. The sensitivity of every country to intrusions on its legal jurisdiction are such that the only workable way forward, and police officers tend to focus on what can be done, is through personal networking: waiting for the politicians to introduce due process will take several lifetimes if the England/Scotland model is any guide.

The cost

To make any changes above the 'tinkering' level will incur significant costs, the least significant of which will be the additional costs of project teams to manage the change. If the reaction to the local government reorganisation in the early 1990s is any guide, police authorities will not go quietly into the night but will go kicking and screaming, defending the need for local democracy and control and predicting the end of local government as we know it. Political parties are only too aware of the fact that it is local government that sustains the activists who are the essential foot soldiers of any national election campaign, and they are very sensitive to this group's need for meaningful involvement in real political activity at a local level between national elections.

In the forces themselves proposals for significant amalgamations or regionalisation will cause massive disruption at middle and senior management level with people trying to position themselves for the new organisation, internecine fighting between factions as groups seek dominance in the new organisation, the demoralisation of those who think or know that they will lose from the change either in actual jobs or career prospects, all accompanied by a planning blight on the forces to be amalgamated in the year or so before it takes place. While this is going on a significant amount of management effort will be focused on the changes rather than on service delivery and any government must ask itself if the game is worth the candle. In terms of policing there are two key questions that may help. Does the government intend to establish some form of regional government? Does the current structure look suitable for the foreseeable future?

If there is to be regional government then it is clear that the service should also be organised on this basis. If that is not intended it is submitted that the democratic deficit would be intolerable and the pull of centralisation would be so strong that the service would become merely an arm of whichever ministry was given responsibility for the police and would end up in the same remote position that the NHS now finds itself.

It is clear from the description given above that the current structure has a considerable number of weaknesses but it is unlikely that they can be corrected by a small number of amalgamations and the forces involved will suffer all of the problems described above with the consequent penalty in both service delivery and political acceptability.

Whatever the future option it is clear that the service must continue the drive to create self-sufficient BCUs with as much budgetary and policy devolution as possible as this will make any subsequent changes easier to manage. It would also be logical for forces to develop as many collaborative arrangements as possible and there are examples of this working success-fully but usually only where the decision is one for the chief constables. Where it is necessary to involve others, the sheer number and rise of those involved, chief constables, the police authorities, the Home Office, ACPO, APA, the Police Federation, the Superintendents' Association, coupled with the bureaucratic machinery used, makes the probability of a successful outcome much less promising. For example, it has taken over six years to develop a nationally agreed uniform. The outcome is limited to a small number of articles of clothing for which the specification appears to keep changing and it is still not in general use. Experience like this make the calls for increasing collaboration more a pious hope than a real expectation.

Issues

1. Although there is no common basis for the existing structure in either size, complexity or democratic congruence, neither is there an agreed ideal model to which the service can move which can guarantee gains in costs, performance or democratic accountability.
2. With all of its weaknesses the current structure has proved to be resilient over a quarter of a century and has shown an ability to absorb considerable change, especially the 'reform' programme of the last seven years.
3. No grounds have been established which show that the amalgamation of a smaller force into a neighbouring larger one will improve performance, no matter how that is defined. Any amalgamation is guaranteed to reduce performance in the short term at least. Such a change will reduce the democratic accountability as long as the size and composition of the police authorities remain fixed.
4. Any 'magic number' of sustainable force size above 2,000 will produce anomalies and a whole host of Procrustean beds.

5. A change to a regional structure would produce cost reductions which, though significant, are not enough in themselves to warrant change. It may take decades rather than years to recover from the performance losses elsewhere.
6. The major justification for a change to a regional model lies in the gains to be made in management and operation efficiency and the ability to formulate and implement policy much more quickly due to the reduction in chief constables and police authorities.
7. A move to a significantly smaller number of forces could improve leadership at both BCU and force level.
8. There is already a significant 'democratic deficit' in police accountability in the larger forces and a wave of amalgamations without a collateral change in police authorities or local government would exacerbate this.
9. Strategic changes in most of the factors that affect crime are the responsibility of local or central government agencies. If the most is to be made of the synergy possible between the service and these agencies there must be a political match of the two structures. The BCU is now a sound model for delivery of police services and would fit with a consistent model for unitary authorities. A move to a regional police model should only be considered as part of a general change to regional government if the overwhelming pull of further centralisation is to be avoided.

Conclusion

As I progressed through the book I have tried to summarise the issues which I think are raised in each of the sections. The purpose of this chapter is to draw together what I believe are the four main obstacles to progress for the service which arise out of the preceding analysis. Those obstacles are, firstly those elements of the culture which constrain change and which resist the adoption of a value system which can deal ethically with improving performance. Secondly, there is a whole plethora of issues around how the service is led and managed. Thirdly, there is a clear need for at least a debate around structure, beginning by considering all of the options and then selecting the best rather than working from the basis of an assertion that some change is needed so let us go for that which is easiest to engineer, i.e. a small number of amalgamations. Finally, there is the need to create new and effective negotiating processes for pay and conditions of service which allow chief constables to play a role which properly reflects their responsibilities.

Culture

Too often when police culture is discussed the only element which is found worthy of mention, is the 'canteen culture', i.e. that which resists change and which rapidly socialises new entrants into accepting poor or bad practice. Such an approach ignores the fact that most elements of the police culture are forces for good rather than evil. There is a 'can-do' culture which in my experience is almost unique to the service. This is reflected in the enthusiasm that is shown for carrying out the task-in-hand, especially when that task is focused on detection or the control of disorder. The service is responsible in both senses. This is exemplified by its attitude to dealing with other agencies, often taking the lead in order to get the job done even where logic, and often statute, state that the other agency should do so e.g. the government drugs strategy. The other side of responsibility is shown by the way that it holds itself highly accountable to the community and responds quickly to criticism e.g. the service's relationship with the Audit Commission. The service is highly resilient to shortage of resources and unreasonable demands on what can be achieved with what there is. Officers at every level show courage, both physical (faced with the threat of violence and personal injury), and mental (dealing with highly disturbing situations or difficult and complex problems where action needs to be taken based on limited information). A service that complies with this paradigm has much of which to be proud.

Those elements of the culture that must be changed are, as is often the case, partial reflections of a strength. Being highly task-focused also means there is an unwillingness to reflect on what has been achieved and how it could have been done better. The very success of the 'can-do' approach has spawned a negative attitude to analysis and research, an element compounded and reinforced by the lack of numeracy skills and poor management information systems. The 'hands-on' approach and respect for operational achievement at every level have bred an approach to learning which is, at its worst hostile, or, more usually, indifferent. As far back as 1983 an American professor on attachment to the National Police Staff College stated that no police manager would read any book on management that did not have the word police in the title (Panzarrella, 1983), in the belief that the police task was unique and that the best learning environment was the 'police university of life'. While the situation has improved since then this is still the case for the majority of police managers at every level.

These features, which are fatal to the prospects of future development if not removed, are deep-rooted and consistent. Their removal will require a continuity of management and a consistency of leadership that is not possible under the current structure. The mere existence of 43 forces makes it impossible to achieve the necessary level of consensus on the way forward and the number of senior posts (chief superintendent and ACPO) make the quick movement through the key ranks of inspector and BCU commander inevitable, especially for the better officers.

Leadership

If the major issue facing the service of the future is to change the culture both in terms of the argument above and in how it deals with diversity, and it is argued here that it is, the key issue is who can do it? There are only three possible candidates; the Home Office, the police authority and the chief constable. It is clear that the Home Office cannot do it. It is not their responsibility, they are too distant from the problem, and they certainly do not have the skills. Neither can the police authority do it. Leadership is very rarely a committee exercise and whilst they do have responsibility for providing an effective and efficient policing service and complying with the requirements of Best Value, operational decision-making and leadership are still at least perceived to be the responsibility of the chief constable. This process of elimination leaves only the chief constable.

If these changes are to be brought about by the chief constable it is worth examining what their powers and room for manoeuvre are in carrying out this task. Almost all issues on pay and conditions of service are determined at national level in negotiations that involve the staff associations, the Home Office and representatives of the police authorities. ACPO are not represented by right on the employer's side, they certainly do not fill a pivotal position. The Home Office as advised by the APA, ACPO and staff associations decides discipline regulations. The new discipline regulations, while they are an improvement on the old, are still complicated and convoluted with an obscure burden of proof whose true meaning is yet to be tested in the courts, and where legal representation is allowed at far too early a stage. Negotiations between individual chief constables and staff are hidebound by regulations and, while it is possible to make some arrangements outside of these, it can only be done with the agreement of staff. Experience shows that the primary driver in these circumstances is benefit to staff rather than to improve service. It would be interesting, since comparison with commerce is usually seen to be the way forward, if a chief executive of a commercial enterprise could be found who:

- Was permitted no part in negotiating pay and conditions of service for staff.
- Could not make any changes in the reward system for outstanding or poor performance.
- Had found that over time their autonomy to operate the business was being gradually eroded.
- Did not have the options of redundancy, early retirement etc, to deal with significant variations in the budget.
- Had to get the board's authority for relatively small changes in the budget.

I am certain that it would be impossible to do so as the ability to influence all of these issues is key to that of leadership and to ensure that accountability for success is matched by the authority to deliver it, yet it exactly describes the position of the chief constable. The tensions created by this are unsustainable over time. The changes in the constitutional position to further diminish the office of chief constable are happening either accidentally, due to other changes in legislation, or by subterfuge because it is believed that the public would not support it. Either way it has created an unhealthy position in terms of the leadership of forces and urgently requires an open debate and clear decision by government on what it requires from the office and what authority it will invest in it to achieve that objective.

Structure

The current structure is an accident of history. It is not underpinned by any logic in terms of size, complexity, or political congruence. Nor is there any model that satisfies these three factors between the status quo and one organised on a regional or national basis. If the focus is on changing the culture in terms of performance and dealing with diversity then there is a need for continuity and consistency in leadership and management style. This is just not possible with 43 forces and is unlikely to be improved in any significant way with the amalgamation of a small number of the smaller forces. Logic dictates that any change that does not affect the larger forces will not change anything of any significance. The change to a regional or national structure would massively reduce the number of senior posts and thus ensure that the better officers stayed in key posts for a much longer time.

The structure would also deal far more effectively with organised crime and with what is currently termed cross-border crime. In addition a large infrastructure would enable the service to deal far more effectively with the concept of direct entry, on either rank or specialism basis, which would significantly enhance the service's ability to deal with diversity. The current situation in forces shows only too clearly the inadequacy of exhortations by HMIC and the governorship of police authorities in delivering on these issues. A final but important point is that further amalgamations will only increase the democratic deficit and further loosen ties with communities. If the service is to improve it is essential that the BCU and the unitary authority become the bedrock, with real accountability to that unitary authority being created for the BCU commander in terms of selection and budget. The combination of these factors, combined with the probability of remaining in posts for a much longer period of time, will enhance and improve local service delivery. It bears repeating however that the police structure must be congruent with the political structure, both in order to provide a system of local accountability which will diminish the pull of centralisation, and to ensure that the police commander at the BCU and regional level can influence those other government agencies whose work is critical to the prevention and reduction of crime and disorder in the strategic sense.

Employment Negotiations

At best these processes can only be described as a mess. On the employer's side those with the highest level of accountability both in statute and in the eyes of the public for delivering the service, the chief constables, have the lowest level of representation and influence. The employer's side is riven with difference and agendas on a civil service, local politician, political party, North versus South basis. The outcome is written in the anachronistic stone of statutory instruments that reduce the ability to negotiate on a local or force basis to near impossibility. Facing this on the employee side is a highly focused, well organised, single minded organisation whose sole function is to negotiate on behalf of its members and which has shown a formidable capability for influencing public opinion. It is in urgent need of radical reform in a way that is precluded by the existence of 43 police authorities.

The Reform Agenda

When looking at this element I am reminded of the old joke of the traveller asking the yokel for directions only to be told that he wouldn't start from here. The police position epitomises the constitutional mess that has been created in local government, firstly by the gradual centralisation of real budgetary power and the creation of unelected and unaccountable quangos, which characterised the 18 years of Conservative power. That has been followed by the same drive for centralised power under New Labour, to which has been added the possibility of parliamentary and electoral reform. Labour has shown itself to be much more courageous in pronouncements than in implementation in the latter with the half-hearted and relatively meaningless reform of the House of Lords, whose representative credentials were not improved by the first batch of 'people's peers'. Regional government is already a reality. It appears to be thriving in Scotland and is making progress, if with less certainty, in Wales. Central government has established a regional footprint that is continually expanding in size and influence. What is not at all certain is where this is all intended to lead us.

A decision to establish regional government would give real clarity, as the political congruence would be inevitable and there would be at least the possibility of having a body of sufficient political weight to counter the ever-pervasive pull of the centre. The danger is that the service may become part of that trend which is already obvious in education, where the structure of local government is left in place but the real power relationship is between the centre and the local service provider. In the health service, the other large and important service provider, the change happened a long time ago. This would be a disaster in terms of democracy and accountability. In the absence of a decision to establish regional government it is difficult to see how an issue of such complexity and constitutional importance as the reform of the governance, leadership and management of the service could be entrusted to any one political party. For all its acknowledged weaknesses the only route that would reassure both the public and the service would be that of a Royal Commission, and even here ACPO and the Home Office would need to exercise an unprecedented degree of co-operation and co-ordination if they are to balance the lobbying effectiveness of the Police Federation.

References

Alderson, J. (1984) *Law and Disorder*. Hamish Hamilton.

Bittner, E. (1975) *The Functions of the Police in Modern Society*. New York, Jason Aronson.

Bossard, A. (1998) Mafias, Triads, Yakuza and Cartels: A Comparative Study of Organised Crime. *Crime and Justice International*. Dec. 5: 6, 30–2.

Bossard, A. (1999) The Basic Principles of Money Laundering. *Crime and Justice International*. Mar. 9: 10, 32.

Buckley, R. (Ed.) (1999) Organised Crime. *Understanding Global Issues*. 99: 1.

Ewing, K.D. and Gearty, C.A. (1990) *Freedom Under Thatcher: Civil Liberties in Modern Britain*. Oxford University Press.

Green, A. (1995) *Fitting up: An Analysis of the Manufacture of Wrongful Convictions*. PhD Thesis, Keele University, The British Library Thesis Service.

Hadley, J.A. (1999) *Policing Post Macpherson: Whiteness and the Valuing of Diversity*. MA thesis.

Her Majesty's Inspector of Constabulary (1998) *What Price Policing?* London, HMSO.

Jefferson, A. and Grimshaw, R. (1984) *Controlling the Constable*. Frederick Muller/The Cobden Trust.

Levi, M. (1998) Perspectives on 'Organised Crime': An Overview. *The Howard Journal*. 37: 4, Nov. 335–45.

Lilley, P. (2000) *Dirty Dealing: The Untold Truth About Global Money Laundering*. London, Kogan Page.

Lubens, V.A. and Edgar, J.N. (1979) *Policing by Objectives*. Hertford, Conn. Social Development Corporation.

MacGregor, S. and Pimlott, B. (1991) *Tackling the Inner Cities*. Clarendon Press.

Macpherson, Sir W. (1999) *The Stephen Lawrence Inquiry. (Cm. 4262-I)* London, HMSO.

Mark, Sir R. (1978). *In the Office of Constable*. William Collins.

Mullin, C. (1997) (5th edn.) *Error of Judgement*. London, Chatto and Windus.

National Association for the Care and Resettlement of Offenders (1999) *Drug-driven Crime: A Factual and Statistical Analysis*. NACRO.

Neyroud, P. and Beckley, B. (2001) *Policing, Ethics and Human Rights*. Devon, Willan Publishing.

O'Byrne, M. (1997) An Improved Service. *Policing Today*. 3: 2, Jun.

O'Byrne, M. (1978) The Right to Silence. *The Police Review.* Nov.

O'Byrne, M. (2000) Can Macpherson Succeed where Scarman Failed? in Marlow, A. and Loveday, B. (Eds.) *After Macpherson.* Lyme Regis, Russell House Publishing. 107–12.

O'Connor, L., Evans, R. and Coggans, N. (1999) Drugs Education in Schools: Identifying the Added Value of the Police Service within a Model of Best Practice. *Police Research and Management.* 3: 3.

Panzarelle, J. (1984) Management versus Policing by Objectives. *Police Journal.* 57:2, 110–28.

Reiner, R. (1991) *Chief Constables.* Oxford, Oxford University Press.

Reiner, R. (1994) What Should the Police be Doing? *Policing.* 10:3, 15–7.

Reiner, R. (1996) *The Politics of the Police. (2nd edn.)* Sussex, Wheatsheaf Books.

Rose, D. (1996) *In the Name of the Law.* London, Jonathan Cape.

Runciman, Viscount. (1993) *The Royal Commission on Criminal Justice. (Cm. 2263)* London, HMSO.

Scarman, Lord. (1981) *The Brixton Disorders 10–12 April 1981.(Cm. 8427)* London, HMSO.

Senge, P.M. (1992) *The Fifth Discipline: The Art and Practice of the Learning Organisation.* London, Century Business.

Sheptycki, J.W.E. (2000) *Issues in Transnational Policing.* London, Routledge.

Singh, G. (2000) The Concept and Context of Institutional Racism, in Marlow, A. and Loveday, B. (Eds.) *After Macpherson.* Lyme Regis, Russell House Publishing. 29–40.

The Royal Commission on the Police (1962) *Final Report.* HMSO.

Vick, C.F.J. (1990) *The Politics of Law and Order.* MA Dissertation. Bramshill Paper.

Waddington, P.A.J. (1993) *Calling the Police.* Hants., Avebury Ashgate Publishing Ltd.

Wall, D.S. (1998) *The Chief Constables of England and Wales: The Socio-legal History of a Criminal Justice Elite.* Aldershot and Dartmouth, Ashgate.

Wilson, J. and Kelland, P. (1982) Broken Windows: The Police and Neighbourhood Safety. *Atlantic Monthly.* Mar. 29–38.

Index

Learning Resources
Centre